You can do it!
Mary Block

"I Can Do It!"

How to Help Children Have a Can-Do Attitude About Life

Pam Golden and Mary Block

Roedway Press
La Quinta, California

"I Can Do It"
*How to Help Children Have
a Can-Do Attitude About Life*

All Rights Reserved © 2004 by Pam Golden and Mary Block

No part of this book may be reproduced or transmitted in any form or by any means, graphic, electronic, or mechanical, including photocopying, recording, taping, or by any information storage retrieval system, without the permission in writing from the publisher.

Roedway Press
La Quinta, California

For information
www.candokid.com

ISBN: 0-9659650-9-0

Printed in the United States of America

This book is dedicated to my husband, John, who taught me how important love is, Amber (my Can-Do daughter), her loving (and lovable) husband Keith and Sammy & Connor, two of the best grandchildren who ever graced this earth.
Pam

This book is dedicated to my husband, Dan, who supported me through the writing of this book, and our son, Michael, who carries on the Can-Do tradition in his life.
Mary

Acknowledgements

Writing this book has been an adventure in using Can-Do skills and a confirmation of their power. I (Pam) began writing a book about parenting, then I had writer's block of the worst sort. I had just met Mary and, after talking with her a few times, I knew she would understand what I was trying to get across. So I asked her if she would like to work on it with me. At that time, I thought it would take about two to six weeks to finish the entire book. Now, two years, three re-writes, hundreds of typed pages and oh so many cups of coffee later, we are ready to go to press!

Our husbands are jumping for joy at the prospect of seeing us without a computer attached at our hips. They are thinking they might get a home cooked meal, too, but we are hoping they take us out to celebrate. Therefore, first and foremost, we'd like to thank John O'Keefe and Dan Block for sticking with us through thick and thin and believing in us so that we could finish this endeavor.

If we weren't parents we wouldn't have written a book on raising kids. So, Amber (Pam's daughter) and Michael (Mary's son), you deserve credit for inspiring us to write this story. You'll both recognize a few memories from your childhoods, we think.

Then, it certainly helps to have siblings who know how to write! Sandy Sims (Pam's sister), a newspaper editor, has been a constant support for Pam's writing and gave time to edit part of the first draft. John Whitechurch's (Mary's brother) love of words and writing talent were instrumental in putting us on the right (write?) path with our book. We truly appreciated all his comments and editing.

Thanks to Chris O'Keefe, Pam's step-grandson. It was his dedication to taking on a challenge that, once again, confirmed the effectiveness of Can-Do Recognition.

And, thanks to Mary's 10-year-old niece, Kaitlin Yates, who helped us bring the Problem Solving example alive. It was her Mom, Lori Yates, who was the catalyst that got us working to finish this book. When she told us about a local educational conference, we turned the flame up to complete our book on time.

We want to thank Cece Whittaker, our copy editor, who was willing to work to help us meet our deadline and give us encouraging feedback.

Pam sends thanks to her wonderful friends, Lynn Centeno, Carol Stanfield, Melody Fleming, Dessa Byrd Reed, Vicki Mills, Wendy Wilson, and Phyl Doppelt for always asking, "How's the book coming?" Your encouragement and support was always uplifting.

Mary sends her thanks to her golfing buddies who understood when she needed to write instead of play. Of course, the principals, staffs, parents and kids who she worked with over the years were the ones who taught her to love teaching.

Last, but not least, we wouldn't be here, if it weren't for our parents, our first teachers. Therefore, we thank them for being our Can-Do inspirations.

Albertine Roed is Pam's 100-year-old step-mother who still inspires Pam and hundreds of people with her lively spirit and her Can-Do Attitude. Pam's father, Ed Roed showed Pam you can become a Can-Do person at any point in your life. When he turned his life around at 43 years of age, he became a man who was admired and respected. He went on to touch the hearts of everyone he met. Lee Roed, Pam's mother, was a single mom whose love and warmth encouraged Pam to thoroughly enjoy motherhood.

Charles and Teresa Whitechurch, Mary's parents, were both educators who taught their four kids the love of learning and the fun of the English language around the dinner table. It was her father, a voracious reader, who always encouraged her to write.

We'd like to acknowledge all the researchers, scientists and child psychologists who have been working for years to find out what is best for kids. Their dedication to children, what they have learned and discovered has benefited parents, grandparents and educators. Scientific findings and practice have taught us how to raise happy and well-adjusted children.

Finally I (Pam), want to acknowledge Mary Block, one of the most positive people I know. I don't think whine or complain are in her vocabulary. After writing on this book for over a year, we realized we needed to change our format, which meant starting over at the beginning. Without skipping a beat, Mary was ready to start again. If ever there was a use for the word 'awesome', it is for describing Mary Block.

Contents

Chapter 1 Loving a Child 1

Chapter 2 Becoming a Child's Number One Fan.... 14

Chapter 3 Love, Appreciation and Respect 21

Chapter 4 Try, Try Again 32

Chapter 5 Connecting With Children 41

Chapter 6 Can-Do Connecting 50

Chapter 7 A Can-Do Attitude 58

Chapter 8 A Secure Bond With a Child 70

Chapter 9 Children's Self-Esteem 82

Chapter 10 Can-Do Self-Esteem 92

Chapter 11 Praising Children 103

Chapter 12 Can-Do Recognition 114

Chapter 13 Constructive Feedback 123

Chapter 14 Problem Solving 132

Chapter 15 Can-Do Problem Solving..................... 146

Chapter 16 The Goal Trap 161

Chapter 17 Can-Do Goals....................................... 176

Chapter 18 We Can Do It!....................................... 189

"I Can Do It!"

Introduction

It was a cooking class in La Quinta, California, that brought Pam Golden and Mary Block together. Finding out across the classroom table that they lived in the same residential community, they decided to meet the next morning to walk off the rich sauces they'd been devouring. During their walk around the community lake, discussions between them revealed a common concern for raising children. Despite their different backgrounds, Pam and Mary soon discovered (after several more laps) that they shared similar practices and beliefs about child rearing.

In May of 1998, Pam appeared on the Oprah Winfrey Show with her daughter to share Pam's remarkable life changing experience as a parent. She didn't want other parents to have to wait until their child's junior year of high school or for catastrophic circumstances to learn valuable parenting skills. This passion to help other parents fueled her desire to share what she had learned by writing a book. Using proven research to substantiate her own parenting skills, Pam discovered she was able to distinguish proven fact from hunch, opinion, and folklore.

Mary's approach to teaching evolved over seventeen years. Her initial years in the classroom were spent trying to maintain crowd control. Teaching the curriculum often took second priority. Over time, she found that her style of listening and talking to children made a significant difference in the way they responded to her. As she learned to connect with children and parents alike, the atmosphere in the classroom changed. Kids were still falling out of their seats, but, instead, it was because they were excited and energized to talk about what they were learning. She discovered learning could be fun and rewarding for children and educators.

Because of Pam and Mary's commitment and desire to share what they learned about raising kids, it was natural for them to pool their ideas. The cooking class ended, but Pam and Mary's new learning adventure had just begun as they worked together creating this book, "I Can Do It!" How to Help Children Have a Can-Do Attitude about Life.

Their hope is, after reading it, you will take away at least one new parenting, grand-parenting, or teaching tool that helps a child build a Can-Do Attitude.

Chapter 1

Loving a Child

"Knowing someone is there for him, no matter what, helps a child build a Can-Do Attitude about life."
— Linda Schaeffer

The rain was hitting the car windshield in large drops. I was straining to see the exit sign as the windshield wipers swished back and forth across the window when my cell phone rang. Who could be calling me so early in the morning, I wondered as I pressed the button to answer my phone?

"Hey, Mom. Guess what?" I heard my son's voice on the other end.

"Chris? Are you alright?" I had just dropped him off at school fifteen minutes earlier.

"I forgot my reading project!" I could hear the panic in his voice.

My heart sank. I took a deep breath and said, "You're kidding! This is the second time you've done that this month. Great way to start third grade!" I could feel the anger building in my voice with each word.

"But, I'll get in trouble with Mr. Garcia if I don't have it," he pleaded.

Exhaling, I said, "Okay, I'll go home and get it."

"Thanks, Mom, love you." He hung up before I could say anything else.

As I headed for home, I remembered my neighbor, Maggie, saying the previous week at the soccer game, "No one ever told me having kids was so much fun!"

That's crazy, I thought. I love my son, but right now being a parent isn't what I call *fun*. Lately, it's been one crisis after another. I was dreading Chris's going to Middle School in a few years. If he can't even remember his homework, I thought, how's he going to handle more independence? I shuddered at the thought.

After I dropped Chris's homework off at his school, I rushed back to work. By lunchtime, I was still feeling annoyed so I decided to call my Mom. Being a parent had always been so easy for her. She took everything in stride and never seemed to stress over anything.

When my Mom answered the phone, I blurted out, "Mom, I need help!" I hadn't planned to start that way, but the words just seemed to tumble out of my mouth when I heard her voice.

"What's the matter, Lisa?" she asked. "You sound upset."

"Oh, Mom, I'm at my wit's end with Chris."

"What happened?"

"For one thing, he forgot his homework again this morning, and I had to drop everything to get it to him. That made me late for a meeting, and my boss almost hit the roof."

"Oh, honey," she said.

"Mom, I thought by the time Chris was in third grade, I wouldn't need to rescue him all the time. On top of that, he spends all his time playing computer games. We fight about his homework every night. I just feel like we're always at odds over something."

"Sounds like you're having a tough time."

"How did you do it?" I asked. "You had two kids, and nothing seemed to phase you. I only have Chris, and

I can't even cope with one kid. Tell me, do you have a Linda Schaeffer Magic Secret for Parenting?"

My mother laughed, "I didn't have a magic parenting wand, and believe it or not, it wasn't the smooth sailing picture you remember. There were many times when I dreamed of escaping to a tropical island."

"I never had any idea you felt that way!" I looked at the phone. Was this *my* mother talking?

"Are you kidding?" she went on. "If I didn't go to the hairdresser every week, you'd see how many gray hairs I really have. Being a parent is one of the hardest jobs in the world."

"I'm finding that out, but, Mom, you always seem to be so calm and wise."

"I don't know about being wise. But, once I accepted being a parent to you and Todd was a huge responsibility and a lot of work, a calmness and change in attitude came over me."

"Wow! What happened that caused that change in you?"

"Well, it was the day Todd almost choked on a piece of hard candy when he was 3 that woke me up."

"What do you mean?"

"Do you remember Danny, the little boy from next door?

"How could I forget? It's like he and Todd were twins, they were together so much."

"That's right. Well, Todd and Danny were playing outside one day and they came inside to ask if they could have some candy. I let them each choose one piece out of the candy jar. The next thing I knew they were back out in the yard on the swing set."

"Was this before I was born?"

"You were 6 weeks old at the time. I went upstairs for a minute to check on you, and I just happened to look out the window. I knew immediately what was happening when I saw Todd gagging on the swing. Danny's swing was still going, but he had gotten off and was standing there, looking at Todd helplessly. By the time I reached him, his face was blue, and he couldn't catch his breath."

"I can't imagine how scary that must have been."

"I still remember thinking—our son is not going to die over a piece of candy! I turned to Danny and yelled at him to run home and get his dad. While he was gone, I turned Todd upside down and shook him, tried the Heimlich maneuver, and everything else I could think of. Nothing was working. I don't know what came over me or how I did it, but I finally just reached way down Todd's throat and pulled that piece of candy out!"

"No wonder you never let us have hard candy!"

"I never bought it again! After the crisis was over, and Todd was lying on the couch shaking with fear, I began to realize that I had almost lost our child over something as small as a piece of candy. At that moment, it hit me what a huge responsibility being a parent is. I vowed right then and there to do everything possible to make sure nothing like that ever happened again."

"Mom, you can't protect your kids from everything every moment."

"That's true. But up until then, I always assumed that your Dad and I were doing the right things. That day helped me realize that we might not always know what the right thing is."

"But how were you supposed to know what the right thing was?"

"That was a biggie for me."

"What did you do?"

"I devoured every parenting book and magazine I could get my hands on, talked to my friends, your teachers, and, even took parenting classes. At night, your Dad and I would discuss what I had found out after we put you and Todd to bed. Sometimes our talks were a little heated, but having different points of view was helpful."

"Really?" I was amazed to hear this coming from my mother. I thought she was just naturally a great mom.

"Then, of course, there was practice, practice, practice. There's lots of advice on the best way to raise kids, but does it work? That's the question. By the time you came along, I had worked at parenting for three years. Your brother gave me plenty of practice."

I laughed out loud thinking of my older brother. "I'll bet Todd gave you a run for your money!"

"But I have to say, it all came together for me at a Westside Community College parenting class. I remember the instructor saying 'A parent should be a child's *'number one fan!'*"

"What does that mean?" I asked.

"I wasn't sure, until he said, 'Knowing someone is there for him, no matter what, helps a child build a Can-Do Attitude about life. That means being your child's *number one fan.*"

"But aren't parents that naturally?"

"We think we are, but often parents get caught up in the hum drum of daily life and forget to let our kids know we are their fans. I realized if we didn't think about it, you and Todd would be grown up before we knew it."

"I think that's where we are with Chris right now. How do you stop that from happening?"

"Your dad and I decided that it was our job to let you and Todd know we were your *number one fans.* So we made sure one of us would be there for whatever you and Todd did at school and after school. Like your games, your plays, and your school nights. We also made sure to hug you lots, read to you, listen to your problems…"

Cutting her off, I said, "Wow! I never thought of it that way, but I always knew you and Dad were there for us. You also made sure we did our homework. Even when I did something wrong, I knew you would listen. In fact, you were the first one I wanted to call when I was upset with Chris today."

"Being a *number one fan* doesn't mean being easy on kids. If you're helping a child build a Can-Do Attitude about life, he needs to learn how to handle problems and be responsible for his own actions. But it starts with you. If you are his *number one fan*, whatever you do will be done in a caring way, even when you're mad at Chris."

"Well, I'm pretty annoyed with him right now and I'm not feeling too loving."

"It isn't always easy to be your kid's fan when he disappoints or embarrasses you. It's especially hard when he doesn't appreciate the sacrifices you make."

"Is that ever true! I don't think Chris has a clue about what he put me through this morning and that really makes me mad."

"Don't be so sure he doesn't appreciate you. I had a life altering moment one time when I thought you and Todd didn't appreciate me.

"What happened?"

"Do you remember when I had to go to San Francisco for a conference? You were in the third grade and Todd had just started sixth grade."

"Oh yeah, I remember, that's when Dad gave us ice cream every night. I'll never forget that."

"I'll bet you won't. But, I had promised to call you every night before you went to bed."

"I remember that because Todd always sat right by the phone so he could be the first one to talk to you. We fought about it every night."

Mom laughed, "Does that ever bring back memories. Well, because this was before cell phones, I had to go back to the hotel to call you. When there were dinner meetings, it was a real pain in the neck. One time, I got up in the middle of a meeting to rush back to call home. When I got through, all I heard was you and Todd yelling at each other. You were so caught up in arguing, you could have cared less about talking to me. I hung up feeling disappointed and hurt."

"I don't remember that."

"But you probably do remember the next night when I didn't call, don't you?" my mom asked.

"Boy, do I ever. After Todd and I fought about who would get to answer first, the phone never rang."

"That night there was a big reception for everyone attending the conference. I was having a lot of fun, and it ran later than I expected it to. When I saw the time go by, I thought, it doesn't matter to you if I call, so why break my neck to get to the phone?

"But it did matter to us."

"I found that out! When I got back to the hotel, there were three messages waiting. Thinking something was wrong, I immediately called your Dad. He told me how devastated you two were. That's when I realized I needed to be your *number one fan* whether I felt like it or not, whether you appreciated it or not. I've lived by that ever since."

"I'm sure glad you're my mom. I wish Chris felt that way about me. I don't think he knows what I had to go through this morning to get his reading project to him."

"Being your child's fan means that you are in touch with your love for him. It doesn't mean always coming to his rescue."

"Are you saying I shouldn't have gone back to get Chris's homework for him?" I asked.

"Well, that's a decision for you to make. Giving him unconditional love and letting him know how important he is to you is not about saving him, buying him what he wants, or even teaching him. It's about letting him be himself and loving him no matter what."

"That's not always easy," I said.

"I know. It takes a lot of time and thought, but after a while, being your child's *number one fan* becomes a habit. Lisa, I'm so glad you called me. I have to run though, because I'm meeting my walking buddy in a few minutes. Remember, we're training for that 10K race that's coming up?"

"Mom, it is so great how you stay in shape. I have to go too. My boss has walked by my office three times already," I laughed. "Thanks for taking the time to talk to me. I do feel better, and you've really got me thinking. I just have one quick question, why didn't you tell me about being a *number one fan* before?"

"I haven't thought about being your fan for a long time. It's so easy to do after all these years."

"I hope I can say the same thing to Chris when he's older. Talk to you later. Love you."

"Love you, too, Sweetie, and good luck with Chris."

As soon as I got off the phone, I jotted down what my mother had said about being a child's *number one fan*. I was determined to take it home, show it to Ted and do whatever it takes to make sure Chris knows we are his fans.

Being a Child's Number One Fan

When you are a child's *number one fan*, it means you are in touch with your love for him. Letting a child know you are his number one fan is a parent's job.

Knowing someone is there for him, no matter what, helps a child build a Can-Do Attitude about life.

Chapter 2

Becoming a Child's Number One Fan

"Maybe our feelings would come more naturally, if we were more in touch with our love for him."
- Lisa Davis

Seeing the light still on in Chris's room that night, I peeked in the doorway. Our dog, Bailey, was snuggled up on the end of the bed, and Chris was absorbed in his Harry Potter book.

"Time to go to sleep," I said as I leaned down and planted a kiss on Chris's head.

"Aw, Mom," he said, but I saw the smile on his face and knew he liked it.

When I went downstairs, I found Ted sitting at the computer in the kitchen. He was working on the bills, but I was determined to tell him what had been on my mind since the conversation with my mother earlier in the day.

"Ted?"

He looked up at me over his glasses. "Yeah?"

"Did you ever think of us as Chris's *number one fans*?"

Turning his chair toward me, Ted said, "What are you talking about?"

"Well, it's something my mom said today. She told me some amazing stuff that I never knew before—like when she realized parenting can be just plain work."

"No kidding!"

"What really got me was when she told me how she and my dad have always worked at being our *number one fans*."

"*Number one fans* for you and Todd? What does that mean?" he asked.

"Well, they were always there for us, no matter what we did. Being a fan is letting your kid know you appreciate him and what he does. It's also supporting him through the good and the bad times. Mom and Dad always tried to go to all our school events and our games, too. Here this is what I wrote down," I said as I took the piece of paper out of my purse.

After reading over what I had written, Ted said, "Well, what's the big deal? We do all that stuff, don't we?"

"It seems like we do, but are we just going through the motions and not really letting Chris know we are his *number one fans*?"

"Well, maybe. I guess I have been so caught up in my new project at work that I haven't thought of anything else for weeks. I can't remember the last time Chris and I went out to shoot baskets together."

"Yeah, and I've felt more and more irritated by things he does. I'm afraid I don't let him know how much I love him. Instead, it seems like I am always telling Chris what he is doing wrong."

"Well, it sounds like you had quite a talk with your Mom today. How did you two get into this whole thing?"

Leaning against the counter, I told him, "This morning, Chris forgot his homework again, and I went all the way home to get it so he wouldn't get in trouble at school. I felt so angry at him all morning because I was late for a meeting. So, I grabbed a sandwich, closed my office door, and called my mom to vent during my lunch hour. That's when she told me about being my *number one fan*."

"I've always known your mom is your fan. I've just never thought of it in those terms."

"Mom never told me about it before because she's worked on it so many years, it's become second nature to her. Another thing she said is how important it is to be a kid's *number one fan*, because that helps him build a Can-Do Attitude about life."

"That makes sense," Ted said. "Having you behind me as my *number one fan* gives me the confidence to put myself out there and try new things."

"So, on the way home from work, I started thinking about Chris. Being a little kid must be hard with two adults constantly on your case to do the right thing. Sometimes we forget what a great kid he is, and he needs to know we feel that way."

"Come to think of it, I used to hug Chris and tell him I love him all the time. Since he has gotten older, I decided maybe he doesn't want his Dad smothering him in front of his friends, so I've laid off even when his friends aren't around."

"Maybe our feelings would come more naturally, if we were more in touch with our love for him. So, I thought we could make a list of things we love and appreciate about Chris. In fact I already started," I said, as I took another piece of paper out of my purse.

I handed Ted the list and he it read out loud:

> *Things We Love and Appreciate About Chris*
>
> 1. *How he smiles with his eyes.*
> 2. *He treats everyone fairly.*

I saw a familiar soft look come over Ted's face. "You're right, he does smile with his eyes, sort of reminds me of my Father. And, you know, he is nice to everyone, even grouchy Mr. Anderson down the street." I smiled, thinking about how Chris did wave at Mr. Anderson whenever Chris was out shooting baskets."

"Let's put this on the computer," Ted said as he began typing. He loves being organized, and I was glad. It sure isn't my thing.

"That's a great idea," I said. "I can have the list with me all the time, and that way it will be easier to keep his special qualities in mind. Also, when Chris does something that drives me bonkers, I could get it out and read it. I think this would help me stay under control and keep things in perspective."

"Yeah. We hope our love comes naturally, but it's too easy to focus more on what kids do wrong. This list would help us stay out of the wrong trap."

I pulled a kitchen chair over to the computer, and together we began to brainstorm what we love and appreciate about Chris.

This is the beginning of the list Ted and I wrote.

Things We Love and Appreciate About Chris

1. How he smiles with his eyes.
2. He treats everyone fairly.
3. He is kind to animals.
4. He's responsible.
5. He likes helping his grandmother.
6. He does his chores.

When we finished our list, Ted looked at me and said, "I guess we haven't raised such a bad kid after all."

"He is a great kid. I just don't want to lose touch with that--ever," I said.

"Me, either."

"You know what? This list is all about our love for Chris. How about making another list of things we can *do* to let Chris know that?"

"That's a great idea," Ted said yawning, "But, it's past my bedtime."

"Okay. Why don't we do that tomorrow night?"

Ted nodded as he saved our list on the computer and printed out two copies. I folded mine and put it into my purse.

Climbing the stairs, we stopped to check in on Chris. Looking into his room, we found him sound asleep, tangled in the blankets with his head on Bailey.

Chapter 3

Love, Appreciation and Respect

*"It's so easy to forget
that kids are people, too."*
-Ted Davis

I was standing at the kitchen sink when Ted came home from work the next night. He gave me a kiss on the cheek, and then hung his jacket on the back of the computer chair. Grabbing the newspaper from the kitchen table, he looked over the front page as he leaned against the counter.

"How was your day?" he asked.

"Better. In fact, I can't believe how making that list of things we love and appreciate about Chris last night changed *my* attitude," I said as I tore up the lettuce for our dinner salad and put it in a bowl.

"What do you mean?" he asked, turning to the Sports section. I couldn't see his face, just the top of his head over the paper.

"Well, Chris came banging in the door after soccer practice today and tracked mud all over the kitchen floor. I couldn't believe the mess he made. When I saw the big muddy footprints leading from the kitchen door to the sink where he was gulping down a drink of water, not only did I *not* get mad, I didn't even snap at him."

"So, you hugged him and said 'I love the way you get mud all over the floor?'" Ted said with a grin, peeking over the top of the paper.

I looked at Ted seriously. "You would have been proud of me. I was able to calmly discuss the problem and work out a solution with Chris."

"Really? What did you come up with?" Ted asked.

"After talking it out, we decided he is going to take off his soccer shoes in the garage and keep them on the shelf by the door. If fact, it was his idea!"

"Way to go, Chris and Mom! Hey," Ted said, putting the paper on the counter, "aren't we going to work on that list tonight--the ways to *show* our love and appreciation for Chris?"

"Yeah. I'm glad you remembered," I said.

"Last night got me going, and all day ideas kept popping into my head at work. But, after your mud incident today, I think we should start the list with: Work out problems with Chris calmly."

"I never thought of working out problems as a way to show love, but you're right. I don't like it when someone jumps all over me. So, why would we treat Chris that way?"

"You're right. It's so easy to forget that kids are people, too. I feel appreciated when someone talks to me respectfully, so I'm gonna to make sure I talk that way to Chris from now on." Ted said as he set down the paper and headed for the refrigerator.

I went on, "You know, respect is so important, I think we should call our new list *How to Show Our Love, Appreciation and Respect for Chris*."

"R-E-S-P-E-C-T," Ted sang as he grabbed me and started dancing around the kitchen. "Sock it to me, sock it to me," he sang on as he swung me around.

I laughed as he landed me back at the sink and danced his way over to the computer, with his best Aretha impersonation, "…that's what it means to me."

Ted began tapping away on the keyboard. So, I went over and stood behind him as Ted began a new page. At the top of the page he typed *"Ways to Show Chris Our Love, Appreciation and Respect."*

"Okay. The first one is *Solve problems with Chris calmly,"* I said as Ted typed, noticing that he added the words *listening carefully*.

"That's great. I really like that *listening* part," I said, "But, you know, listening to what someone else has to say is so important that it should have its own number."

Ted easily moved the *listening* part down to its own line and a number 2 popped up in front of it. "I just love technology," he said.

"Oh, and don't forget to put *hugging* down. I want to make sure we do that. And saying *'We love you'*, and *'We're glad you're part of our lives'*. We've gotta have those."

"Whoa, pardner! I can't type that fast," Ted said as he tapped away and added them to our list. When he finished, Ted looked over at the oven. "Whatever you're cooking sure smells good. When are we eating?"

Just then the oven timer went off, and I took the chicken casserole out, setting it on the stove. The cheddar cheese had melted on the top to a nice golden brown.

"Chris," I called, "time to set the table!"

Ted saved what he had been typing and shut down the computer. "Let's finish this after dinner," he said.

I agreed as Chris came into the kitchen, kicking an imaginary soccer ball with his stocking feet.

This is the list Ted and I came up with after dinner.

*Ways to Show Chris Our
Love, Appreciation and Respect*

1. *Solve problems with Chris calmly.*
2. *Listen carefully to Chris.*
3. *Hug Chris lots.*
4. *Say "We love you, and we're glad you are in our lives."*
5. *Give Chris our full attention without interruption or 'multi-tasking'.*
6. *One of us will read to Chris every night.*
7. *After reading, go over Chris' Golden Moments of the Day.*
8. *Display Chris' pictures, artwork, trophies, and accomplishments throughout the house.*
9. *Call Chris if you can't be home for dinner, are out of town, or have to work past his bedtime, making sure both of us communicate with him every day.*

When Ted and I finished the new list, we looked it over. "This is exactly what I needed to make sure I'm letting Chris know I love, appreciate and respect him. Let's print out a copy for each of us," I said.

Ted clicked on the print icon, and two copies shot out of the printer. He hand me a copy as he looked over his. "You know, seeing these in print makes me aware of how much you do with Chris."

"Well, you're right. I've done most of these things with Chris before, but I haven't been consistent and that's the problem. Something always seems to come up, and the next thing I know I'm trying to hurry him to go to bed, and then it's the next day. We get caught up in the same cycle over and over."

"Now that we've taken the time to think about it, and made this list, I think that's going to help us break out of that busy cycle."

"I think so, too."

"In fact, I'm excited about doing more of these things with Chris," Ted said as he looked at the list. "I'd like to be the one to read to him tonight and go over his Golden Moments of the Day."

"That would be great. I'm afraid that's one of those things I've let slide lately," I admitted.

"I've heard you and Chris talking about Golden Moments, but what are they?" Ted asked.

"Oh, you'll love it. Chris and I started doing Golden Moments of the Day when he was in first grade. It was the day his fish died, and he was still very sad about it when he went to bed. So, we talked about pets dying and how sad we feel when that happens."

"Oh, yeah. I remember the day you were cleaning Goldie's bowl, and she jumped out and went down the drain."

"I was shocked the way it happened so fast. I reached for her, but she was down the drain before I could do anything. I felt awful, knowing I'd have to tell Chris what happened when he got home from school."

"That was a pretty sad night at our house. Goldie had swum her way into our lives," Ted said as he pretended to wipe his eyes.

"Oh, Ted, you're so dramatic. But, I think you get what I'm saying, don't you? After Chris and I talked about Goldie, I wanted him to fall asleep with some good thoughts. So, I asked Chris to tell me some good things that happened that day. I remember him telling me he got to take the ball out for recess. There were a few other things he shared with me, too. Then I shared my Golden Moments of the Day. Just talking seemed to lift his spirits. Chris and I decided to share at least one bad thing and one good thing that happened every day. We started calling these our Golden Moments of the Day."

"Named after Goldie, right?" Ted asked laughing.

"Yeah. Chris thought it up. And I think he had a good idea, because sharing the bad things along with the good helps him learn both are part of life. After all, things didn't go so well for Goldie that day."

"Rest in peace, Goldie," Ted said respectfully as he bowed his head.

"Enough about that fish," I said glancing at the kitchen clock. "It's almost Chris's bedtime, and Mr. Reader needs to get ready for his first performance."

"I'm not sure I can live up to your reputation, but I'll sure try," Ted smiled.

As I was folding up my list to put in my purse, a spark went off in my mind. "Oh, I almost forgot. I wanted to add Family Night to our list."

"What's that? Don't we have Family Night every night?" Ted asked.

"Well, having a specific Family Night is a little different. Maggie told me about it. She said she and the girls pick one night each week reserved just for them to do something together—no one else is invited. Maggie said everybody in the family has to commit to saving that night—it's like a sacred pact between them."

"Hey, that sounds like a good idea. It would make sure we do something fun together each week," Ted sounded enthused.

"I thought you'd like it," I said.

"Okay. So how does it work? Is it the same night each week?"

"It usually is, but it doesn't have to be."

"Well, what do Maggie and the girls do?"

"Maggie said they talk about ideas, and each person gets a turn deciding what the family will do. Sometimes they go out to eat or cook together. Other times they go to a movie or a ballgame. Once they had 'Game Night', and they played Monopoly and Clue for hours. The girls loved it!"

"Imagine that —no TV or computer games—and they still had fun together," Ted said. "Are you sure about that?"

"Yeah."

"Let's ask Chris to help us plan our first Family Night," Ted said.

"He could even be the one to choose what we do first. Let's have a Family Meeting tomorrow night during dinner to plan it."

"You're on," Ted said as he started singing, "We are family…"

As I watched him dancing and singing his way out of the kitchen and up the stairs on his way to read to Chris, I started to think Maggie might be right. Having kids could be fun after all.

Chapter 4

Try, Try, Again

"Maybe this was going to be harder than we thought, but I was determined to give it another try."
- Lisa Davis

When we told Chris that we were going to start having Family Nights, he was less than thrilled. Ted and I were disappointed when Chris said, "You mean it's going to just be the three of us? Jason can't ever come?" We had been so excited, we'd just assumed he would be, too. This being a *number one fan* business was getting off to a rocky start.

Ted and I looked at each other across the dinner table. Ted said, "Well Chris, how about if you pick what we do for our first Family Night?"

"And, how about this Friday night for our first one?" I added.

After talking about it, Chris decided we should make homemade pizza together and eat ice cream sundaes while we watched a video—easy enough.

On my way home from work Friday, I stopped at the grocery store to get everything we needed for the pizza and sundaes.

As Chris carried the groceries in with me, he asked if he could help make the pizza dough. Maybe he's warming up to our evening together after all, I thought. When the dough had risen, I called Chris to come and help me punch it down in the bowl, one of his favorite parts of making pizza.

Once we had rolled the dough into a ball and flattened it out, Chris started tossing it up into the air like he'd seen those guys do in the pizza kitchen windows. He couldn't get it to flatten out like they do, but I could tell he was having fun and that was what was important.

"Mom, don't forget Dad and I like pepperoni and sausage on ours," Chris said.

"I've got it right here," I told him opening the refrigerator and reaching into the meat drawer.

When Chris asked where the sauce was, I couldn't believe it was the one thing I had forgotten to buy. But it was no problem for Chris. He thought it would be great to use barbecue sauce instead. At that point, I was happy to agree.

As we were spreading the dark brown sauce on the dough with the back of a spoon, the phone rang. Since both of us were up to our elbows in dough and sauce, I picked up the phone with my sticky finger tips and nestled it between my ear and shoulder.

I knew it was bad news as soon as I heard Ted's voice. I could tell he was still at work when I heard machinery running in the background.

"Honey, you won't believe this," Ted said. "One of the production machines has been on the blink all afternoon, and the guys just got here to work on it. I can't leave until they're finished because I have to let the plant in Cincinnati know when we are up and running. I'm sorry. This is the first chance I've had to call you."

"How long is it going to be?" I asked.

"Well, it looks like it'll be a couple more hours, at least," he said.

I felt as bad as he did, and I knew how stressed he must be. "Don't worry about it. Chris and I will go ahead and bake the pizza and start the video," I said looking over at Chris who was putting so much pepperoni and sausage on the pizza that the sauce had almost disappeared.

When Chris heard me, he stopped and looked up at me with disappointment in his eyes.

"I'm really sorry, Lisa, I had been looking forward to tonight. Save me a piece of pizza, would you? And can I talk to my buddy?"

I motioned Chris to come over to the phone and held it up to his ear because his hands were covered with more sauce than mine.

I heard Chris say, "That's okay Dad, I understand." But I could tell the fun had gone out of his voice. He ended with, "Yeah, love you too, Dad. See ya later."

We put the finished pizza in the oven and made a quick trip to the video store that was just around the corner. Searching every rack, neither of us could find anything G-rated that Chris hadn't already seen. We went home empty-handed.

The minute Chris opened the kitchen door, we both gasped. There was trash all over the floor. Following a trail of chewed paper up the stairs, we found Bailey licking the pepperoni package under Chris' bed.

Just when we finished picking up the trash Bailey had scattered everywhere, Chris said, "Is something burning?" That night, Chris and I feasted on burnt barbeque pizza while we watched our own copy of "The Lion King" for at least the 100th time.

The one good thing that happened that night was when Chris and I treated ourselves to the biggest, whopping sundaes you have ever seen. We wolfed them down while we watched the video.

Chris was asleep, curled up on pillows on the floor, when Ted finally got home close to ten o'clock. He came in looking exhausted. "Sorry to miss our first Family Night together, but there was no way I could leave any earlier. What's to eat? I'm starving!" he asked. I offered him the rest of the pizza, but when he saw it, he wasn't hungry anymore. Later, I saw him sneak out to the kitchen for a bowl of cereal.

Maybe this was going to be harder than we thought, but I was still determined to give it another try.

It wasn't until Wednesday night, when the three of us were driving home from Chris' soccer game that Ted brought up the idea of trying another Family Night.

"Maybe this time we should try a Family *Day*," I suggested. I could still taste that burned pizza.

"Who gets to pick what we do this time?" Chris wanted to know.

"I think since your Dad couldn't make the last one, why don't we let him pick?" I said.

"Hmmm . . ." Ted was quiet for a minute, "This is going to take some real thought," he said.

"Come on Dad, pick something good," Chris urged.

"I know," Ted suddenly blurted out. "We could go fishing. Can't we fish in the lake at the park?"

"Yeah that's cool! Jason caught a fish there last week with his brother," Chris said. "Can we ride the boats, too?"

"Well, if we catch enough fish for dinner," Ted said, giving me a wink as he pulled into our driveway. "How about if we have a picnic after fishing, and then we'll go for a boat ride?"

"Hey, that sounds like fun. I'll be the photographer," I volunteered. All I could see were squirming worms and smelly fish, but I didn't want to put down Ted's idea, so I bit my tongue and tried to be enthusiastic.

When Ted turned the engine off, we all got out of the car. I went inside the house, but Ted and Chris stayed in the garage, searching for the fishing poles and bait box that had once belonged to Ted's father.

Sunday morning came before I knew it. Ted and Chris came downstairs all decked out in fishing vests and hats. They had lures hanging everywhere and looked like they had just stepped out of an advertisement for fishing gear. "Where did you find those?" I asked, laughing as I took the first picture.

"These belonged to my Dad, too," Ted said. "I thought we could fool the fish into thinking we know what we are doing."

I followed them out to the car feeling underdressed for the premier event. So I grabbed a straw hat as we walked past the laundry room, hoping I looked like a photographer and fishing would remain a spectator sport for me.

As we piled out of the car at the park, Ted and Chris carried the bait box and three poles. I knew what that meant. They were expecting me to fish, too. I was reluctant at first, but I gave in when they insisted this was a family event and everyone had to at least try.

I was watching the bobber on my line floating in the water. It seemed harmless enough. But all of a sudden, the bobber disappeared under the water and something started pulling on my pole. I couldn't believe it. I didn't know what to do, I started jumping around and yelling, "I've got a fish! I've got a fish!" and almost dropped the pole right into the water.

Ted and Chris came running over and stood next to me. "Way to go, Mom!" Chris said.

I tried to hand the pole to Ted, but he wouldn't take it. "Oh no, this fish is all yours," he said as he calmly told me how to reel the fish in. As soon as the fish was out of the water, Chris came to my rescue and took it off the hook. I gratefully watched him throw it back into the lake and surrendered my pole to the bank. I spent the rest of the afternoon photographing the tiny bluegills Ted and Chris reeled in time and again. I secretly thought they were all the same fish, but I didn't say anything.

After the guys had had enough of fishing, we found a grill and picnic table where we could cook our hot dogs and make s'mores. I'd forgotten how good food tasted grilled over an open fire and how good graham crackers, chocolate, and toasted marshmallows were all smashed together.

"I don't think we've been here since Chris was in a stroller," I said to Ted as we wandered through the park and over to the boat rental shed.

"That was fun. Can we do it again?" Chris asked on the way home.

I smiled. Even though our first attempt had been a royal flop, I was so glad we hadn't give up, and I couldn't wait to show my mother the pictures we had taken.

"Hey Mom, it's your turn to pick what we do on our next Family Day," Chris said. "What are you going to choose?"

"Hmmm .,., I've been wanting to go to that new shopping mall that just opened up," I said.

"No way!" Ted and Chris both yelled at the same time.

"Don't worry, guys. I'll pick something that you at least sort of like to do!" I said leaving them in suspense.

Chapter 5

Connecting With Children

"If you understand how a person sees a problem, then you are in a position to help him work through it."
- Linda Schaeffer

"I can't believe I blew it, and it was all going so well," I lamented to my mother as she sat down at our kitchen table. "We've had some really fun family times together lately."

"I know you have. I still have that picture on my refrigerator of Chris and Ted in crazy fishing outfits, holding up those tiny fish," she said laughing.

"Yeah, and were they ever surprised when I chose going to a basketball game for my Family Day last weekend. It was the first professional game Chris has ever seen. And Ted didn't even know I had bought the tickets. It was right after that weekend that we seemed to take a step back."

"What happened?" my mother asked as I poured us each a cup of coffee and sat down at the table with her.

"Well, last Monday night I was working on the computer in the kitchen, and Chris was studying at his desk in the family room. All of a sudden, I heard him groan loudly. I looked up just as he threw his Math book on the floor, stomped over to the couch and turned on the television."

"Oh!"

"I went right over and said as calmly as I could, 'Chris, you know the rules. No television until your homework is done. Please go over there, pick up that book, and finish studying for your test.'"

"That doesn't sound too bad," Mom said.

"I was proud of myself for keeping my cool because one of the things we've been working on is solving problems calmly."

"Did it work?" my Mom asked.

"That night it did and on Tuesday, when I asked Chris how he did on his math test, he said, 'Okay,' so I figured everything was fine. But, on Thursday, when I was emptying all the trash baskets, I saw a crumpled up piece of school paper in Chris's trash can. There were Math problems on it. So, I picked it up and looked at it. It was Chris's math test with a big fat D at the top."

"Oh, no." My mother looked disappointed.

"I knew Chris was outside shooting baskets with Jason, so I went right out, sent Jason home and told Chris to come inside. I had the Math test sitting right here on the kitchen table. "What's this?" I asked him, pointing at the test.

Chris just looked down at the floor and mumbled, 'My Math test.' He wouldn't even look at me."

"This isn't good," my mom said.

"You better believe it. That's when I lost it. You know how I can't stand being lied to! I yelled at Chris and told him he was grounded until further notice. He wasn't allowed to watch TV, play video games, or listen to CD's until he brought up his Math grade. I sent him up to his room, which is where he is right now on this beautiful Saturday morning."

"Sweetheart, do you know why children lie?" my mom asked gently.

"Of course. They don't want to get punished."

"That's right. But, when children don't tell you the truth, you can't help them solve their problems. All of their attention is focused on being mad at you, feeling unloved and feeling sorry for themselves."

As my mother was talking I could picture Chris up in his room, lying on his bed pouting, in total silence.

"I'll bet you Chris is not spending one second figuring how to bring that up that D in Math," my mother continued.

"I can pretty much guarantee he's not working on his Math, and I don't know how to make him. I wish he'd asked me for help with his Math and maybe all this wouldn't have happened."

"Sometimes kids don't ask for help because they're embarrassed, scared, or feel stupid when they run into a problem. In order to trust you with their problem, kids have to feel safe with you."

"How do I get Chris to feel safe with me?" I wanted to know.

"You do that by *connecting* with him."

"What do you mean, *connect*?" I asked

"*Connecting* means listening and . . ."

Cutting off my Mom I said, "But I *do* listen to him. That's even on the list Ted and I made and I've really been working at it."

"*Connecting* is more than just listening. When you *connect* with a child, for that moment, you almost become one person, seeing the situation the same way he does," she explained.

"I never thought of trying to see what was happening from Chris's eyes. He was struggling with his Math, and I wasn't listening at all. Instead of asking him what was upsetting him, I just assumed I knew."

"That's right. You can't help Chris if you don't know what he's dealing with. If you understand how a person sees a problem, then you are in a position to help him work through it," my mom said as she finished her coffee.

"I forgot something, too. We were supposed to work through problems calmly *together*, but I didn't include Chris in any of the problem solving. I just got so mad when he acted that way that I lost my temper."

"It happens to all of us. Kids have a way of getting under our skin sometimes. But when this happens, it's one of the best times to connect. You seize the moment to *connect* and go with it."

"I guess I could use some more practice at *connecting*," I said.

"It does take practice. I remember one time when you were about 3 years old. I walked into the living room and there you were rubbing toothpaste on the antique dining room table my mother gave me. I started to yell at you, but I saw the intense look on your little face and I stopped. When I asked you what you were doing, you looked up at me with those blue eyes and said, 'I'm making Mommy's table all shiny.' When I asked you why you were using toothpaste, you said, 'Cause you do.'"

I could picture the beautiful table that had always been in my mother's dining room. "Oh! I'll bet I know what happened. To me, the tube of toothpaste must have looked like the tube of polish that you still use on that table."

"That's right," Mom said. "You thought you were doing something wonderful for Mommy. If I had yelled at you, you would have been so hurt. Instead, I took the moment to see what was happening through your eyes.

Because I realized you were trying to do something nice for me, the anger disappeared. Then I could show you the right way to take care of the table. Problem solved. That's what *connecting* is all about."

"I want to start *connecting* again with Chris," I admitted. "But I don't know how to begin."

"You can *connect* with Chris anytime. For instance, when you are riding in the car and talking, standing in line at the grocery store or when you read to Chris at night. In fact, the more you *connect* when things are going well, the more likely you will be able to *connect* and work problems out in difficult times."

"Like when he gets angry and frustrated," I added.

"A perfect time to *connect*," my mother smiled. "If Chris believes you want to understand the situation and how he feels about it, he's more likely to trust you with his concerns."

"I'm not sure I would know exactly what to do," I said.

"The first thing is to listen carefully without judging or interrupting. Then, to make sure you understand his point of view, you can restate what Chris said, in your own words. If you didn't get it, he can tell you. And, sometimes it's important to share your thinking and reasoning. That kind of exchange builds the connection between you."

"I guess I have some work to do. I feel so much better. Thanks Mom." I gave her a hug as she got up to leave. "So, we were *connecting* just now, weren't we?" I asked. My mother smiled at me, and hugged me back.

"It's one of my favorite things to do with you," she said as she opened the front door, letting in the brisk fall air. I watched my mother walk down the front steps.

As I wrote down what my mother had said about connecting, in the back of my mind, I was thinking about Chris upstairs in his room, grounded for life.

How to Connect With A Child

1. As you listen, give your full attention without judging or criticizing. (This can be really hard to do.)

2. Rephrase and repeat in your own words to make sure you understand and he knows you understand.

3. When appropriate, share your thinking and reasoning.

4. Use words like 'oh', and 'tell me more' to encourage him to talk freely.

Chapter 6

Can-Do Connecting

*"Then, the word 'connect' popped
into my head. Instead of blowing up,
I decided to give Chris a chance
to tell me why they did it."*
- Ted Davis

The following Saturday afternoon, I was sitting at the computer researching places to go for spring break, when Ted came in from the garage. He had a confident look on his face. "Now, it's your turn to be proud of me," he said.

"What are you talking about?" I asked.

As he bent over and gave me a kiss on the cheek, he explained, "I think Chris and I just connected—right out there in the garage!"

"No kidding!" I couldn't believe it. Ted had seemed so skeptical when I had told him what my mother had said about connecting. "Where's Chris now?" I asked.

"He's over mowing Maggie's lawn," Ted answered with a big grin.

"He is? Did she ask him to do it? She usually likes to do it herself for the exercise." I could hear the hum of our mower outside. "What happened out in the garage, Ted?"

"Well, I was working on the car, changing the oil, and Chris was just hanging around, watching me," Ted said looking through the refrigerator. "Do we have anything for lunch?"

"You talk, and I'll make you a BLT," I offered, knowing it was his favorite sandwich.

Ted said, "I'll be glad to fry the bacon, but I've got to wash my hands first." He went over to the sink as I shut down the computer.

"Okay, now give me the scoop," I said, taking the ingredients out of the refrigerator and setting them on the counter.

"Well, Chris was sitting on the garage floor, watching me empty the oil. I had just emptied the last of the oil into the recycling can, when out of nowhere Chris says '*We* did it!' It was so strange. I didn't know what he was talking about. So I asked him, 'Did what?' Then he revealed the big secret. He told me that he and his cousins were the ones who rang Maggie's doorbell."

"What?" I asked.

"Remember last week when Maggie called you so frightened because someone rang her doorbell at 9:00 at night? But no one was there when she went to the door?"

"Yeah. She was really freaked out. Oh no! Chris and his cousins did that? I can't believe it!" I felt so upset, hearing Ted's words.

"Well, they did. It was the night your sister, Jane, dropped her boys off for a sleepover because they didn't have school the next day.

"I remember," I said, thinking back to that night. Ted had even gone next door and walked around Maggie's backyard with a baseball bat. It had been so dark out there, it made me shiver.

Ted was shaking his head, and I could tell he was remembering that night, too, as the smell of frying bacon filled the air.

"How did they do it, Ted? Right after Maggie called, I found the boys in the family room, watching a video. Oh! They must have come inside while I was on the phone with her." It all seemed so simple now. "When I asked them if they had seen anyone over by Maggie's house, they said they hadn't. I didn't even suspect them!"

Ted said, "It sure surprised me. I didn't think the boys would do something like that."

"Plus, I can't believe Chris lied again! That really makes me mad."

Ted agreed, "When he was telling me about this, I started feeling angry, too. But then, the word 'connect' popped into my head. Instead of blowing up, I decided to give Chris a chance to tell me why they did it."

"What did he say?"

"Well, he explained how he and his cousins had wanted to play a harmless joke. So, they snuck over and rang Maggie's doorbell and ran back over here as soon as they saw her front light go on. He said they got to our house just as the phone was ringing. You're right, so they tried to act like they had been watching TV the whole time. Chris told me his stomach has been hurting ever since it happened, but he's been afraid to tell us. You know what he said next?"

"I can't imagine," I said as I spread mayonnaise on the bread and began to put Ted's sandwich together. The hum of the mower sounded closer, so I knew Chris was now in Maggie's backyard. I looked out the kitchen window and saw Chris and the mower making a turn.

Ted took the sandwich over to the table and sat down. "Chris said he wanted to tell me the truth but he didn't know how to start. He said he decided to tell me the second I finished emptying the old oil into the recycling can. I guess that's why he said it so abruptly."

I left the window and started to laugh at the thought of Chris waiting for that last drip to happen. Then I said, "It's not really funny."

"No, it's not," Ted said. "And, he gets that now. I really held onto my cool, and I did that thing about rephrasing what he said in my own words to make sure I understood him. I tried to not make any comments or judgments, either. Saying 'Oh' helped a lot. Chris looked so relieved after he told me the truth, that I almost felt sorry for him."

I went over to the phone. "I've got to call Maggie and tell her. I know she'll feel so much better when she finds out it was just Chris and his cousins. She's been leaving the outdoor lights on every night since this happened."

"You don't need to do that," Ted said. "Chris took care of it himself."

"He did? You mean he's told Maggie already?" I couldn't believe it all had happened while I was on the computer!

Ted smiled. "Yeah. We talked about why it was wrong and why Maggie was so afraid. I don't think he'll be pulling that prank again. What really gets me is that if I had yelled at him or punished him, I know he wouldn't have learned nearly as good a lesson as he did from our talk."

"Maybe you're right," I said as I opened a bag of potato chips and offered them to Ted. "But don't you think he should have some sort of punishment?"

"Well, I asked him about that. And, he offered to go over and apologize. He was only over at Maggie's for a few minutes when he was back in our garage. He asked me if he could use our mower to do her lawn. I guess he offered to mow her lawn for scaring her so much. I thought that was pretty cool of him to think of that on his own."

"That's amazing," I said, feeling a little better about the whole situation. "Nice job, Dad."

"Thanks. I think it worked out pretty well. Connecting really helped me and Chris this morning," Ted said as he took a bite of his sandwich.

"I see another list in our future. I think connecting deserves its own page," I suggested.

"We're going to be listed out pretty soon," Ted said.

I sat down at the table with Ted and looked at him. "I'm glad we've made our lists. They help remind us where to focus with Chris. I'm amazed at what we've learned recently about raising kids. Looks like we still have some work to do, though."

"Hey, aren't you and Maggie going shopping and out to lunch?" he said, looking at the clock.

"You're right, and I've got to get ready. I told her the other day that we've been working on our parenting skills. She couldn't believe she was the one who got me started in the first place with her comment about how much fun it is to have kids. Maggie also says parenting is often two steps forward and one step back. I can't wait to hear what she thinks about how this prank all worked out!"

"Parenting is a lot harder than I thought it would be," Ted said.

"I think we're on the right track though, Mr. Connector," I said as I gave him a big hug on my way upstairs to get ready.

Chapter 7

A Can-Do Attitude

"I felt a surge of excitement as I realized this could fit right in with the other pieces of the parenting puzzle Ted and I were putting together."
— Lisa Davis

I felt a little awkward when I saw Maggie, standing outside in our driveway, talking to Chris. He was leaning on the lawnmower, and I couldn't see his face. As I went out and joined them though, I was glad to hear their friendly banter about our local high school football team.

"Here's my favorite shopping buddy," Maggie said as soon as she saw me, giving me a hug. "Didn't Chris do a great job on my lawn?" she asked, pointing to her yard.

"You really made it look good," I told him. "Thanks for doing that. I left you a sandwich on the counter for lunch. Maggie and I will be home later. Maybe we can get tacos for dinner."

"Yeah, that sounds good," Chris said as he pushed the mower into its spot in our garage. He waved at us as he went into the house.

"Well, the whole doorbell thing really surprised me," I said, getting into Maggie's car. "Both Ted and I were shocked to hear that Chris had done it. Sorry to put you and the girls through that ordeal."

"You don't know how relieved I am that it was just Chris and his cousins." She breathed a sigh of relief. "Now we can rest easier tonight."

As she drove, Maggie listened intently to the story of Chris admitting the prank to Ted in the garage that morning. When I finished, she said, "Chris must have been feeling so guilty all week. He was so cute when he came over and told me, Lisa. You would have been proud of him. Then when he offered to mow the lawn, I couldn't say 'no' because I could tell he wanted to make it up to me some way."

"Ted told me he and Chris had quite a talk. Hopefully, he learned something from this, especially how serious a prank can be!"

As Maggie turned her car into the mall parking lot, she said, "He's a good kid, Lisa. It's really fantastic that you and Ted are working so hard to make sure you're doing the right thing for Chris."

It was my turn to breathe a sigh of relief. Maggie seemed to be more interested in shopping now than the doorbell prank because she began telling me about the great sales she had seen in the morning paper. Coupons in hand, we took on the mall.

A few stores later, we decided to grab a quick bite at the food court. It wasn't easy to find an empty table amidst the throng of hungry shoppers, but we finally did. As Maggie put her tray down, she said, "You and Ted have done so many things right as parents. When I became a single parent, it dawned on me how much *I* would be impacting my daughters' lives because they would be spending most of their time with me."

"Weren't the girls preschoolers then?" I asked as I searched for another piece of chicken in my salad.

"Yeah. That was before you and Ted moved next door. Rachel was three and a half, and Jennie was just starting Kindergarten. What really got me thinking about parenting was the school newsletter I found in Jennie's backpack. Each newsletter had articles about specific parenting skills written by professionals."

"I used to read those, but lately I haven't had the time," I admitted.

"Well, the article that really hit home with me was about the impact adults have on children's lives. It said that kids are always watching and learning from us. Right after I read it, I overheard Jennie scolding Rachel. She sounded just like a short version of me. I decided I needed to be more aware of what I said and did in front of the girls," Maggie said with a chuckle. "That's when I started reading everything I could about parenting."

"How did you do that when you were raising the girls all by yourself and working full time?" I was sure Maggie had found some extra hours in her days!

"At first, it was overwhelming. Some authors seemed to contradict what the others were saying. But when I realized there *is* a difference between what has been *proven* to work and what people *think* might work when bringing up children, it opened the door for me."

"What do you mean 'proven to work.'?" I asked.

"Well, there are lots of parenting books written by well-meaning people full of techniques that worked for them. I was determined to find something that worked for a number of people. I didn't want to be experimenting with my girls' upbringing."

"I'm not quite sure what you mean."

"Well, the FDA doesn't approve a medicine until it's been tested and proven to work for most people. I wanted the same assurance for the way I was raising my girls, if it was possible."

"Oh, I get it. You wanted parenting skills based on research?"

"Absolutely, and I found some. There are a few basic principles that help children develop a Can-Do Attitude."

When Maggie said 'Can-Do attitude, I really perked up. That sounds like something my mother said to me recently. But I wasn't quite sure what she meant by a Can-Do Attitude?"

"Well, after plowing through tons of parenting books and articles, it seemed to me that several authors were saying the same thing using different names for it. Some psychologists called it 'optimism' or 'resilience.' Others called it 'mastery-oriented thinking' or 'self-efficacy'. All those big words were too complex for me. I liked what they were saying, so I put their lingo into my own words and Can-Do Attitude really captured it for me."

Thinking for a moment, I said, "Hmmm. If a kid had a Can-Do Attitude, would that mean she's a "Super Kid" who does everything right?"

"No, she's not a 'Super Kid' at all. Kids with a Can-Do Attitude make lots of mistakes. But they learn from those mistakes. A child with a Can-Do Attitude is secure in who he is. He thrives and flourishes in life, takes risks and knows that with effort and guidance, he can accomplish any goal."

"This sounds like something that could help Chris. Do you think he could learn to have a Can-Do Attitude?"

"Absolutely," Maggie said. "Oh, and most important, problems can really send kids under for a long time, but when a child has a Can-Do Attitude she bounces back from problems faster because she understands that she can do something about it."

I felt a surge of excitement as I realized this could fit right in with the other pieces of the parenting puzzle Ted and I were putting together.

"This fits right in with what Ted and I are working on with Chris! Tell me more. How do I start? What do we do?" I felt desperate and excited at the same time. I told Maggie about the night Chris got so frustrated that he threw his math book on the floor. "I'd love to see him develop a Can-Do Attitude about his school work," I admitted.

"You know how Chris has all the confidence to work and try new moves on the soccer field?" Maggie asked. "I'll bet he doesn't give up when he makes mistakes out there."

"You're right. I've seen him stick right in the thick of things and just try another way to get the ball down the field. Nothing stops him."

"In soccer, Chris definitely has a Can-Do Attitude because his attention is on *what he is learning*. I used to see him in your backyard practicing for hours. Sometimes he got a little frustrated, but he didn't give up. He knew he just needed to practice more, learn a new kicking strategy, or soccer move. We all have our priorities in life. A person can have a Can-Do Attitude in certain areas and not in others."

"But how can I get Chris to have a Can-Do Attitude in Math? He loves soccer. If he could just transfer even half of that soccer effort into Math, he'd sail through that class and life would be a lot easier for all of us."

"When a child knows that learning anything is a step-by-step process, he can transfer that knowledge into what he wants to accomplish. This works for soccer or math."

"I need to write this down, so I can tell Ted what you said today, Maggie." I had an unused paper napkin and found a pen in my purse. As soon as I was ready, I asked Maggie to tell me again what a Can-Do Attitude is. This is what she said.

A Can-Do Attitude

A child with a Can-Do Attitude is secure in who he is. He thrives and flourishes in life, takes risks and knows that with effort and guidance, he can accomplish any goal.

A child with a Can-Do Attitude:
- Loves learning
- Bounces back from problems faster
- Sees mistakes as a chance to learn
- Persists through roadblocks
- Seeks challenges energetically

Looking at what I wrote, I said to Maggie, "It sounds great, but, how do I help Chris learn this?"

"From all my research, I found two areas adults can work on to help a child have a Can-Do Attitude. The first area involves the parent/child relationship. The second covers specific skills children can learn."

"I think Ted and I could handle two things," I said. "Can you tell me more?"

"Well, the parent/child relationship is about making sure you have a loving and trusting bond so that there is a foundation to work from," Maggie explained.

"My Mom just told me about this. She calls it being a child's *number one fan.*"

"Oh, I like that. You'd be surprised how many adults don't know how to build that secure bond with kids. If we don't know we need to make an effort, we are disappointed when the bond with a child isn't there."

"You're so right," I said. "That bond with Chris had been missing for a while, but since Ted and I have been working at it, I feel so much closer to Chris now."

"Well, once the bond is there, you have the foundation to work on the Can-Do skills which are learning what it takes to achieve goals, problem solving, and goal setting.

"Those are three areas I've never thought about teaching Chris. Isn't that more like teaching kids how to think instead of what to do?"

"Yes, it is. I was surprised myself. When I joined a Can-Do Parenting Group, I discovered other parents who had the same concerns I did. Our goal is to help kids have the skills they need to navigate successfully through life."

"What parent wouldn't want that? But how can you make sure that happens for kids?" I was a little doubtful.

"Well, being in a group really helps. We read and discuss what parenting experts have to say. We share what works and what doesn't. Sometimes we take field trips and go together to hear speakers. I guess what I like the best is knowing that we are all in this parenting thing together—out there trying to do what's best for our kids."

"I don't know if I would be that comfortable sharing with just anybody some of the things Chris has done— the doorbell prank and throwing his Math book. I'm afraid they might think we're bad parents!"

Maggie gave me a friendly pat on my arm. "One of the great parts of being in the group is we feel comfortable openly sharing our problems, because we promise not to criticize or to take stories home. It's wonderful to be able to laugh together at some the things our kids do and say. It puts parenting in perspective. Would you like to come with me sometime?"

"Yeah, I think I would and Ted might, too. Oh! It's not on Monday nights, is it? I'd never be able to get him away from football."

"No way. We were careful to stay away from Mondays. We want as many parents as possible to be able to be there. In fact, the next meeting is this Tuesday night."

Checking my watch, I realized how much time we had spent talking. "Whoa, I didn't mean to take up all our shopping time," I said feeling guilty.

"I didn't mind at all. Isn't parenting our most important job?" Maggie got up and emptied her tray in the trash can.

Ready to find some more bargains, I said, "I want to know more about this group, but I definitely think it's time *we* work on our shopping skills."

"Well, that Sale sign in the Macy's window has my name written all over it," Maggie laughed.

As the two of us picked up our bags and headed for the store, I thought about what Maggie had said. Maybe a parenting group would be helpful for Ted and me. I knew there was more we could be doing for Chris. Wait until Ted heard about all of this! And he thought we were just shopping.

Chapter 8

A Secure Bond With a Child

"It's not just the good times with our kids that bring us closer. Sometimes it's the bad times that give us the opportunities to bond with them."
- Min Lee

Ted was working in the yard when I got home from our shopping trip. I was so excited about what Maggie and I had talked about that I didn't even take my bags into the house. I just set them down in the garage. I couldn't wait to tell Ted about the Can-Do Parent Group.

I was disappointed when he said, "Why don't you go to the Parent Meeting and tell me about it when you get home." Then he went back to raking the leaves into a pile.

Waiting a minute, I said, "Ted, I can understand why you don't want to go. I sort of felt that way when Maggie told me about it," I said. "But I thought we were working on this together for Chris."

"We are, and I think we're doing a pretty good job. What happened with Chris over the prank he and his cousins pulled proves that." Ted stopped raking the leaves and turned to me, "I just don't think we need a bunch of other people telling us how to raise our son."

From the look on Ted's face, I knew he had made up his mind. There wasn't any point in pressuring him into going with me.

So, when Tuesday night came, I got ready to go to the meeting while Ted and Chris cleaned up after dinner. The meeting was going to be at the Lee's house several blocks away, and Maggie was going to ride with me. As I drove down the street, she told me how the meetings rotated from house to house, and whoever was hosting the meeting was the leader for that night.

After we parked in front of the Lee's, I noticed Maggie was carrying a book. Walking up to the front door, she went on, "At each meeting we talk about a specific topic that relates to helping our kids develop Can-Do Attitudes. Everyone comes prepared to share about an article, book, or excerpt they've read."

"Oh, so that's why you brought that book. Is it okay that I didn't read anything?" I was feeling a little bit uncomfortable already.

"Oh, of course, Lisa. The reason I brought this book is because we have a rule that what we use and talk about has been tested and proven to help kids."

I said, "I like the idea of parents finding research about kids, then talking about it before they use it."

"It's really changed the way I do some things with my girls. I'm so glad you came, Lisa. Tonight we're talking about kids' self-esteem. It should be lively. There are so many different opinions about that."

"We've really been working on that with Chris. I praise him every chance I get. Ted and I really want him to have high self-esteem."

Holding up the book, Maggie said, "Boy, was I surprised to read what creates self-esteem."

I was just about to ask her what she meant when Min Lee opened the door to welcome us. I had seen Min at different school events, but I had never met her. One of her sons was in Chris's class, and as Min shook my hand she said, "Oh, it's so nice to meet Chris's mother."

Walking into the family room, I noticed it was filled with people who were talking and laughing. Recognizing one of my neighbors, I waved, and there was one of the fourth grade teachers from Chris's school, sitting next to her husband.

Maggie and I each got a cup of coffee from the kitchen and found two empty chairs. After a few moments, Min stood up in front of the group.

"Welcome," she said with a warm smile. People began quieting down and gathering up their books and articles. "Before we get started tonight, I'd like to take a moment to introduce some people who are here for the first time."

I was one of three new people, and as we introduced ourselves, we each told a little bit about our families. When it was my turn, I shared how Ted and I had been working on our parenting recently and how Maggie's description of a Can-Do Attitude really fascinated me. "So, here I am," I ended with.

Min started the discussion by saying, "The last time we were together, we talked about how creating a 'secure bond' with your child, lays the ground work for a Can-Do Attitude.

My ears perked up when I heard the term 'secure bond.' That's what Maggie had said we needed to work on first with our kids.

Min went on, "For those of you who weren't here last time, this is what we mean by a 'Secure Bond'," she said as she pointed to a flipchart on the right side of the room.

Secure Bond

A secure bond is a healthy and caring relationship between an adult and a child. A child who bonds successfully with a parent, a grandparent, a teacher or other socially responsible adult has the best opportunity to grow into a productive person.

In order to bond, children need to have:
- Meaningful opportunities to feel lovable, capable, and important
- Skills for successful interaction with others, whether social, academic, or behavioral
- Recognition and appreciation for their contributions to family, school, or community

---

Min explained that at the previous meeting the group had discussed developing a Secure Bond through meaningful opportunities for children to feel lovable, capable, and important. She went on to say we would be discussing the other two points—skills and recognition—in future meetings.

As I listened to Min's explanation, I realized that that was what Ted and I had been working on with Chris by being his *number one fans*. I was glad to see we were on the right track. Then a man in a plaid shirt waved his hand.

When Min called on him he stood up and turned to the group, "I sure found out what a *meaningful opportunity* was last weekend with my six-year-old," he said.

Min turned to him and said, "Carlos, tell us what happened."

"Well, I was driving home from the grocery store Sunday afternoon with my son in the back seat. I happened to look in the rearview mirror. Andy's face was *covered* with chocolate!"

Everyone laughed at this.

Carlos went on, "When I asked him what he had been eating, he looked at me with those big innocent eyes and said, "Nothing.""

We all laughed again.

"Then I saw a Butterfinger wrapper in his hand. I couldn't believe it. I remembered that he had asked me to buy him the candy bar when we were standing in line at the store. But, I had said 'No.' When I saw the wrapper in Andy's hand, I knew he must stolen it," he said as he threw up his hands.

I could see the anger in Carlos' eyes as he was talking.

He went on, "I started to really lay into him. But then the discussion at our last Parent Meeting popped into my head. All of a sudden, I didn't know what to do. If I yelled at Andy, I was afraid I would break the Secure Bond I had been working so hard on, but I couldn't let him get away with stealing either. How could I punish him and show Andy I love him at the same time?"

The woman sitting on my left said to Carlos, "I know what you mean. I worry about doing something that will make my daughter hate me forever. What did you do?"

"Well, I took three deep breaths to calm down, like we practiced at our last meeting, and thought for a moment about it. I was so mad, I wanted to take away Andy's bike until he was in high school."

I smiled as I thought about how I had grounded Chris for lying and figured this must be a common reaction parents have.

Carlos went on, "But I figured that taking his bike away probably wouldn't teach him why stealing is wrong. So, I decided this might be the time to try out some of the stuff we've been talking about. All the way home, Andy and I talked about why we don't take things that don't belong to us."

"Way to go, Carlos, keeping your cool," Pat Moore, the fourth grade teacher said.

"Thanks, but I knew talking wasn't enough. Andy needed to learn the right thing to do. When we got home, the first thing we did was clean the chocolate out of the car and wash his face."

Maggie laughed as she whispered to me, "That probably took an hour."

Carlos continued, "Then Andy and I went into his room and sat on his bed. Putting my arm around him, I explained that he had to pay the store back for the candy bar. He didn't like that at all. So I asked him how he would like it if someone just came in and took his basketball and never brought it back."

"That's a good way of explaining," Min said.

"I could tell Andy understood because big tears started running down his face. Then Andy got down off the bed and slowly walked over to his piggy bank. He brought it back and began shaking the coins out onto his bedspread. He had been saving every penny to buy a special baseball card, and this would put a huge dent in his little nest egg."

There was a big "Awww…" from everyone in the room.

Carlos laughed. "Yeah, I felt so bad watching the little guy, I almost let him off the hook. After all, it was such a small thing. But I knew I was helping him develop a Can-Do Attitude and learning to be responsible for what he did is a big part of that. I knew I couldn't let anything pass."

Listening to Carlos made me think about Chris. I knew I had to keep in mind what was best for him and not get hung up on wanting him to like me or be his pal.

Carlos continued, "Andy stuffed the money into the pocket of his jeans and together we went back to the store with the wrapper in his hand. I gotta tell you it was hard on me, too. Not only did I have to work it out with Andy, I missed most of the Raiders' game.

That time everyone said "Awwww…" for Carlos.

"But as I watched Andy dig the money out of his pocket and put it on the counter with the empty wrapper, I knew we were doing the right thing."

I looked around the room and could see other parents were shaking their heads in agreement that Carlos was doing the right thing for Andy.

Carlos started to sit down but then stood back up, "What really got me was when Andy brought me his favorite book to read that night. As he crawled up beside me on the couch, I knew our bond was still there. You know, I think it's even more secure than before. I never thought something like this would make Andy and me feel closer."

"Carlos, your story helped us see that it's not just the good times with our kids that bring us closer. Sometimes it's the bad times that give us the opportunities to bond with them," Min said.

Then a young, dark-haired woman who had been sitting quietly on the couch turned to Carlos and said, "You did a really good job with your son. I have trouble disciplining my daughter because she always ends up feeling badly about herself."

"Well, Andy felt bad, but he got over it fairly quickly," Carlos admitted.

Pat, looked at Carlos and said, "I think the way you handled it was what made the difference. You didn't criticize Andy, instead you helped him understand the problem, learn from it and solve it. You were firm about what needed to be done and kind at the same time. I'm sure Andy felt better about himself in the long run."

Carlos looked thoughtful. "Yeah, I don't think he would have felt very good about himself if he had gotten away with stealing. Even though he is only six, Andy knew he had done something wrong."

Someone started to clap, and soon everyone joined in the applause.

Min smiled as she said, "Maybe this is a good time to take a break before we get started on tonight's topic. There are plenty of snacks on the table in the back of the room. Help yourself to coffee, soda or water. Why don't we start again in about ten minutes?"

As Maggie and I made our way over to the snack table, I said to her, "I wish Ted had come tonight. He would have loved that story Carlos told about his son."

Maggie said, "Yeah, I can't believe how he turned it around."

After hearing Carlos's story, I couldn't wait to hear what other parents had to say about tonight's topic. Looking around the group, I was glad to be there.

Chapter 9

Children's Self-Esteem

"Seeing her do that step by herself convinced me nothing I could say would give her that same satisfied look of accomplishment."
- Tracy Johnson

It wasn't long until everyone was seated again. Min began by saying, "Let's get started talking about tonight's topic. Who would like to put down the main points of our discussion?"

Min's husband, Ben, said, "I'll do it," as he made his way over to a flipchart that had been set up next to the fireplace.

"Any brave people who'd like to share what they've read about self-esteem?" Min asked looking out at the group seated around her living room.

A few hands went up and Min turned to Pat Moore. "Pat, do you want to be first?"

"Sure." Pat said as she stood up. "Well, as a parent and a teacher, I have to say I was really surprised by what I read about self-esteem. At school, we've been encouraged to boost kids' self-esteem by always telling them how great they are and what a good job they're doing. Yet, I could never figure out why some kids with high self-esteem don't do as well they should."

"Really?" Min commented.

"The mystery cleared up when I read the research. In the book I chose, there were two types of self-esteem, *earned* and *unearned*."

Min asked, "What's the difference between the two?"

"Well, if self-esteem isn't earned," Pat said, "it can cause problems. When children have unearned self-esteem, they aren't realistic and expect to do well without putting in the required effort."

A man sitting on the couch had introduced himself earlier as Phil McCoy, a grandfather, who was raising his grandson. "What causes that?" he asked.

"It happens when we try to boost our kids' self-esteem to protect them from feeling badly or failing," Pat said.

"Can you give me an example?"

"Sure," Pat said. "Take a child who doesn't make the select soccer team. If we say, 'That coach didn't know what she was doing,' 'you really were the best one,' or 'that was unfair, you were better than Timmy,' we do our children a disservice. They don't learn how to deal with reality."

"What do you mean, not learn how to deal with reality?"

"When we make excuses, blame someone else or try to make what happened okay, the child won't learn he may need to improve his skills to reach his goal," Pat said.

Min spoke up. "That makes sense. How do we teach kids to deal with reality?"

Pat replied, "I can tell you how I've handled that in Math class. Kids were always asking me, 'Why did you *give* me this grade in Math?' So, one day after six kids asked me that question, I decided to turn it into a lesson so kids could see where their grades came from. I gave each child a calculator and his or her grades. Right there in class, they added up their scores and averaged them. You should have seen their faces. All of a sudden there was a flash of recognition, when they understood they *earned* their grades themselves."

"Did that make a difference?" Phil asked.

"Absolutely!" Pat said. "Once kids realized they were in control, they became more conscientious, more careful and did better. Now I have them average their grades every quarter. These kids are taking responsibility for their grades."

Maggie added enthusiastically, "And those kids will have *earned self-esteem.* No one can ever take that away."

Before Maggie finished speaking, Tracy Johnson, who I recognized as the wife of Chris's scout leader, had her hand up in a flash. Min called on her, "Tracy, it looks like you want to say something. Go ahead."

"That's exactly how it happened with my 9-year-old daughter, Breanna," Tracy said. "She begged me to let her take tap dancing lessons. I finally gave in because she wanted to do it so badly. But I couldn't believe it—after a month, she wanted to quit."

"I think a lot of us have heard that before," Min added. I saw other parents nodding in agreement with Min.

Tracy smoothed back her hair and continued, "Yeah. I didn't want Breanna to give up so soon. I figured all she needed was a big boost of self-esteem. So I began telling her what a wonderful dancer she was. I really laid it on thick. Every chance I got, I would say 'Oh Breanna, you're so graceful.' I truly thought I was helping her."

Min asked, "Did it help?"

"Not one bit," Tracy shook her head. "In fact, it became a battle to get her to go to tap, and I had already paid for the classes."

"Ohhhh," everyone groaned.

"Then I started reading this book," she said, holding up a book with a yellow and blue cover. "I couldn't believe it. It was as if the authors were writing just to me! Listen to this," Tracy said as she opened the book and read, "'The way to increase a child's self-esteem is not to feed her empty phrases or to praise her for accomplishments that are not *real*, but to equip her with skills so she can earn self-esteem herself."

"You're right. It's just like what we were talking about." Min said.

"So I immediately quit telling Breanna she was a fabulous dancer!" Tracy said.

The group laughed at that.

"I asked her why she wanted to quit. At first Breanna said 'I just don't like it.' She finally admitted, 'I'm no good at tap. I can't do it.' When I saw how frustrated she was, I was determined to help her."

Several people said, "Go Mom! You Can Do It!"

Tracy laughed and went on, "Since I had paid for the whole month, I suggested that Breanna at least finish the classes for the next 3 weeks. I told her I would help her. She didn't jump for joy, but said she'd go until the end of the month."

Min asked, "Do we have another budding tap dancer in our midst?"

"Not quite," Tracy said with a smile. "I'm not tap dancing with her, but I did help Breanna set up a time and place to practice at our house. Then we put a schedule on the refrigerator. She's really had to work at it. But she's practiced every day, and she's making progress."

"Is she going to stick with the tap lessons?" Min wanted to know.

"Well, I'm not sure. Last week when she was trying to learn a new step, she told me, 'This is hard, Mom.' But her attitude changed when she finally got the step. She went around dancing for anybody who would watch. Seeing her do that step, convinced me nothing I could say would give her that satisfied look of accomplishment. She'd earned it! I have to admit, this has been a learning experience for both of us."

The whole group burst into applause. Tracy bowed and sat down with a big smile.

Min summed it up perfectly when she said, "So, what we've learned tonight about healthy self-esteem is that it's earned. It isn't something you can give someone. As parents, though, the best thing we can do is equip our kids with the skills needed for doing well in life."

"That's exactly right," Maggie said as she held up her book again. "In this book it says, 'Healthy self-esteem has a clear formula. Do well in the world and you will feel good about yourself. Get good grades, make friends, hit the ball, write a poem, solve a problem and you will feel proud of your accomplishment and yourself. The feel good part of self-esteem is the result of doing well.'"

"So how do we equip kids with what they need to do well and earn their own self-esteem?" Pat Moore's husband, Steve asked.

"Just as Tracy did," Maggie said. "It sounds like Breanna thought she was going to learn to tap dance overnight."

Tracy added, "Yeah, she thought she'd be right up there with the top dancers in no time."

Maggie continued, "Tracy, when you helped Breanna set up a scheduled time and a place to practice, she learned that being a great tap dancer takes dedication, patience, and practice."

"Now I get it," Phil said. "This applies not only to dancing, but to any worthwhile challenge we take on. So, Pat, when you talked about teaching kids to deal with reality, you meant teaching them they are the ones responsible for achieving their goals."

Pat smiled at him, "That's exactly what I meant."

As Min turned to see what Ben had written she said, "Both Pat and Tracy's examples helped us understand that healthy self-esteem must be earned. Ben, I like your heading, Can-Do Self-Esteem."

As we looked over at the chart, Ben said, "Thanks. I figured we needed to differentiate between unearned and earned self-esteem. I hope I caught all the main points."

Can-Do Self-Esteem

Can-Do self-esteem is *earned* by the child. It comes as a result of his or her own efforts.

The best way to increase children's self-esteem is to equip them with skills needed for accomplishing their goals and doing well in life.

Kids need to know it takes time, dedication, patience, and practice to accomplish any worthwhile goal.

"Ben, I'm impressed," Steve Moore said. "You were really listening. You got every point down. I can take it home, type it up and e-mail everyone copies. That way we can work on teaching our kids how to earn their own self-esteem before the next meeting. By the way, where is the next meeting?"

Min said, looking over at Pat, "You won't have far to go because it's at your house."

I smiled to myself as I saw Steve's eyes getting bigger. Obviously, he hadn't known that Pat had volunteered to have the next meeting at their house while he was in the kitchen getting coffee.

"Oh, I guess this is how Pat plans to get her 'Honey-Do's' done," Steve said, laughing as he sat down.

Min smiled and went on. "Our topic for next time is about how to praise and criticize children effectively. Find out what you can and see you the first Tuesday of next month at the Moore's house. Steve would you add your address and directions to the e-mail you're sending out?"

"Sure," Steve answered.

Walking to Maggie's car, after saying goodbye to Min and everyone else, I felt charged with energy. I knew I had to drag Ted to the next meeting, whatever it took.

Chapter 10

Can-Do Self-Esteem

*"The best way to help a kid earn
self-esteem is to teach him how to
master skills so he can achieve his goals."*
- Lisa Davis

It seemed like the crack of dawn the next Saturday morning when Ted and I crawled out of bed and woke Chris up. It didn't take long for the three of us to get dressed, grab some granola bars, pile into the car and head for Chris's soccer game.

When we got there, Ted took the folding chairs out of the trunk and handed them to me. It was our turn to bring the oranges and water for the kids. I carried the chairs while Ted dragged our cooler out onto the soccer field where Chris's team was warming up.

Chris ran ahead of us and joined the other kids on the field with their coach, Mr. Faheed. As Ted and I set up our chairs, we chatted with the other parents on the sidelines. There was a cool breeze coming across the field.

When the game started, I saw a really tall boy from the other team running along side Chris in the middle of the field. Ted saw him, too.

"Hey how old do you think that kid is?" he said out loud. "He can't be in third grade! Hey, John, let's ask his coach for his birth certificate," he said joking to the father sitting next to him.

Jose, one of Chris's teammates, passed the ball to Chris. I looked over at Ted, and he was intently watching Chris quickly moving the ball down the field. Suddenly, the ball was gone! The swarm of kids was now moving in the direction of the other goal. "What happened?" I asked Ted.

"That tall kid got the ball away from Chris. I can't believe Chris gave it up so easily," Ted said, sounding irritated.

Now I could see the boy Ted was talking about. He was headed for the goal on the other side of the field. We watched as he made a perfect pass to a teammate who scored a goal, and the parents from the other team went crazy.

As Chris's team got into a huddle, ready for the next play, I saw Chris was sitting on the bench all by himself. From the way he was holding his head in his hands, I could tell he was disappointed he had let his team down. Ted must have seen Chris, too because Ted was shaking his head.

"Chris is such a good player. Don't worry, he'll be back in before you know it," I said, looking at Ted. "They all take turns playing." Chris did play again that half, but he never gave it his all. In fact, he seemed to shy away from the ball, which was totally unlike him.

Ted and I saw Mr. Faheed talking to Chris during the half time. Since we'd brought the oranges, Ted took them over to the team. I watched as Ted hung around, and I could tell he was trying to hear what the coach was saying to Chris.

Ted came back and sat down next to me. "Well, the coach sure wasn't happy with the way Chris has been playing," Ted told me.

When the whistle blew to start the second half, Chris wasn't out on the field with his teammates. My heart sank. I knew how much he wanted to be out there playing. As I watched him, I was proud of the way he still cheered for his team.

After the game, though, Chris's chin was scraping the ground as he came over to where we were sitting. "Aw, it's just a game," Ted said, giving Chris a pat on the back, but I knew Ted was hurting inside right along with our son.

"That big kid was all over me," Chris said. "I couldn't get rid of him, and then Mr. Faheed got mad and yelled at me."

Ted had a pained look on his face as he listened to his son. "Chris, you're one of the best players on the team," he said.

"Dad, I was lousy today."

Ted tried to console Chris, "It just wasn't your day. You'll get it back."

"No, I won't."

I could tell Chris was really down on himself. I just wanted to hug him and make him feel better. I asked myself, would that be for him or for me? Then I knew he needed more than his parents' comforting. So, I racked my brain, trying to remember what we had learned about self-esteem at the last Parent Meeting.

Ted gathered up the chairs, and Chris carried the empty cooler as we walked silently across the field to our car which was now almost the last one in the parking lot.

As I climbed into the front seat, it came back to me! Self-esteem comes from within a person and is the result of his own efforts. How could I use what I had learned the other night to help Chris now, I wondered. Maggie had explained that we could help our kids by teaching them skills to help them do better.

I decided to give it a try. So I asked Chris who was in the backseat, "Chris, I know you're not happy with the way you played today. Is there something your dad and I can do to help you get ready for next week's game?"

"Sure, Chris. We can practice together, if you want," Ted added.

"Naw. It wouldn't help," was Chris's answer. I turned around and saw Chris staring aimlessly out the back window.

"What do you mean? You're a great player. In fact, you're one of the best on the team. Mr. Faheed doesn't know what he's doing," Ted said.

"Hey Buddy, just because you didn't play well today doesn't mean you can't get better with practice," I said to Chris.

"But I have practiced a lot," Chris shot back.

"How can I get it into your head that you're a terrific player?" Ted was getting agitated.

"But, I'm not…"

We rode for a few minutes in silence. I took a deep breath. "Maybe you were surprised today by the size and speed of that big kid," I suggested. "But, that doesn't mean you can't learn some moves to help you get around him the next time. It won't just happen, though. You'll have to work at it. Remember when you were in Kindergarten and you didn't want to wait at the bus stop with the bigger kids?"

"Yeah."

"Well, we talked about it. You even practiced walking up to them. Remember the day you finally did it?"

"That was the scariest day of my life." Chris was beginning to sound more like himself.

"You didn't know it, but I was watching you from our upstairs bedroom window," I told him. "It was so cute when the bigger kids let you into their circle."

"Yeah. They were really cool to me after that day."

I looked over at Ted. He had become quiet while Chris and I had been talking. I knew he was listening. "So, Chris, what do you think you need to practice before the next game?" I asked him.

Chris waited a few moments then said slowly. "I guess I need to practice moving the ball with my feet. That's what the coach said."

"Do you think that would help?"

"Yeah. That big kid shouldn't have been able to get the ball from me so easily. I mean, he's big, but that shouldn't matter, should it, Dad?"

"No, not really," Ted admitted. "Footwork is more important than size in soccer. Remember when you first started playing, and we got that soccer net and tied it between the two trees in the backyard. You used to practice for hours out there—all by yourself most of the time."

"Gee, I forgot about that net," I said. "Didn't we use it for the fish pond game at the school fun fair one year?" I could still see it hanging up while the kids hung fishing poles over it in the school gym.

"Where is that net?" Chris wanted to know.

"I think it's up in the rafters in the garage," Ted said looking at Chris in the rearview mirror.

"Do you think we could put it up?" Chris asked.

"Well, the trees have grown, but I think we can find some rope that would work," Ted said. "Yeah, I'm sure we can. Let's see if we can find it when we get home. Would you like me to practice with you, Chris? If you can learn to move the ball around me, you'll be able to get it around any big kid that comes along."

"Do you think I could get it around Billy Thompson who plays on the Select Soccer Team?" Chris was starting to sound excited about playing soccer again.

"Yeah, even Billy! Maybe we can talk your Mom into making pancakes while we get the net up." Ted looked at me smiling.

"Chocolate chip pancakes?" Chris asked.

"Sure, if someone hasn't eaten all the chips," I answered looking back at Ted.

I turned around again. Chris was still looking out the window now with a look of determination. Already I could see a change in his self-esteem in the few minutes we had been in the car.

He had to be the one to practice for next week's game, but we could give him the support he needed by putting up the net, telling him we appreciated his efforts to improve, and by letting him know we weren't disappointed in him as a person. As Ted turned down our street, I was beginning to think this wasn't going to be such a bad day after all.

After breakfast, Chris cleared the table and asked if he could go outside and start practicing with the net he and Ted had put up. I rinsed the dishes and handed them to Ted. As he loaded the dishwasher, he said to me, "What you said to Chris this morning made a big change in his attitude. He was so upset after the game that I didn't think he'd ever want to play again, and there he is out in the backyard practicing already."

"Yeah, I'm glad it worked out that way, too," I said, letting out a sigh as I sat down at the breakfast bar.

"How did you know what to say? He definitely listened to you."

"Well, I thought about the Parent Meeting the other night. Since our purpose is to help kids have a Can-Do Attitude about life, self-esteem was an important issue to consider. We learned that *healthy* self-esteem has to come from a person's own efforts. The best way to help a kid earn self-esteem is to teach him how to master skills so he can achieve his goals. That's why I was trying my hardest to get Chris to realize he could improve his soccer skills with practice, and that failure isn't fatal. In fact, like someone said the other night, 'Kids need to fail. If all they ever do is win, they don't learn how to handle failure.'"

Ted's eyes widened. "I never thought about it that way. We try so hard to protect our kids from failure, yet that's how they learn. I've never mastered anything without some kind of failure or mistake."

"That's the way I learn best. Remember all my cooking fiascos?"

"How could I forget!" Ted laughed. "When I felt so bad for Chris today, my first instinct was to do whatever I could to help him feel better about himself. But I can see now that when I was trying to say things to make him feel better, it wasn't helping him."

Chris came running into the house through the garage, "Hey, Dad, when are you coming out?"

"I'm on my way, Buddy," Ted said, putting away the last dish. He walked to the backdoor and turned around. "By the way, Lisa, when is the next Parent Meeting?"

"It's the first Tuesday of every month, which makes it in about 3 weeks from now," I answered.

"Think your Mom could come over and stay with Chris, if we both go?"

"I'll call and ask her tonight."

"Is the meeting going to be about self-esteem again?" Ted asked, standing in the doorway.

"A little bit, because we start by talking about how the information from the last meeting has helped our kids have a Can-Do Attitude. Then we move on to our new topic. Next time it's on using praise effectively with kids. I've already downloaded several articles about praise and kids from the Internet."

"Using praise with kids—that could be interesting. Count me in," Ted said as he went out the garage door.

Chapter 11

Praising Children

"Our words should be like a magic canvas upon which a child cannot help but paint a positive picture of himself."
-Haim Ginott

Over the next few weeks, Ted and I worked to stop flattering Chris. Instead, we concentrated on helping him be more independent in accomplishing his goals.

I was thinking about the changes we were working on when Ted came home from work. "Hey, Lisa, what did the doctor say about Chris?" he asked as he gave me a kiss. I had phoned Ted earlier that afternoon to let him know the school nurse called me at work, saying Chris had a fever.

"Because his temperature wasn't too high, Dr. Jenkins told me to keep track of it and bring Chris in tomorrow if his temperature doesn't go down. I think it's just the flu that has been going around the school."

"Poor guy. Should I go up and see him?"

"That would be great. I was just taking him some 7-Up to settle his stomach," I said, handing Ted the glass.

I was in the kitchen, putting a roast in the oven, when Ted came in with the glass of 7-Up still in his hand.

"Chris was sound asleep," he explained. "Bailey is curled up next to him with his head on Chris's pillow. They look like twins," Ted said laughing.

I could picture the two of them together and smiled. Bailey was definitely taking care of his best friend. "I'm so disappointed because we won't be able to go to the Parent Meeting tonight," I said.

"Oh, you're right! And after all that reading we did. Believe it or not, I was anxious to share what we learned and hear what the other parents found out about using praise with kids." Ted actually sounded disappointed, too.

"Well, you could still go, if you want to," I said. "I can take care of Chris."

Ted took a big gulp of the 7-Up he was holding. He looked at me and said, "I hate to leave you alone."

"Honey, don't worry about it. Chris and I will be fine, and after all, this is for Chris. It would be nice if one of us could go tonight, but I'm really beat. If you went, you could at least find out what other people have to say about using praise effectively."

"Yeah," Ted said. "I guess I could go. But, if I do go, I'll need to write down some notes. Some of what we read was really surprising. There's no way I'm going to remember it all on my own."

"Honey, that's a great idea. Why don't you sit down at the computer, and you can make your own personal Cliff Notes while I put a salad together," I said as I took a head of lettuce out of the refrigerator.

"It's a deal. If you'll help me with the main points, I think I'll be fine," Ted said.

"Well, didn't we mark certain parts in the articles we thought were important?" I set the lettuce on the counter and went to get the pile of printouts we had been reading. Turning to the page where I had left a Post It® note, I read out loud, *"How a child is praised can directly affect whether a child gives up easily or is motivated to keep working on a problem."*

"That was a shocker for me," Ted said. "I couldn't believe a *few* simple words can change a kid's motivation. Okay, so what is the right type of praise?"

"This article says, *'the single most important rule is that praise deal only with the child's efforts, strategies and accomplishments, not with his character and personality.'*"

"You know, I didn't understand that when we first read it, and I still don't get it. What's the difference between praising a kid's personality or his efforts, strategies and accomplishments? To me, praise is praise."

"It says here that *'praise should mirror for the child a realistic picture of his accomplishments, not be a Madison Avenue image of his personality. Our words should be like a magic canvas upon which a child cannot help but paint a positive picture of himself.'*"

"I know we read that before, and it sounded so easy, but now I'm not sure how you do that." I could see the confusion on Ted's face.

"Well, I think that means, if Chris cleans up the garage, and we said, 'You're terrific for doing that', we would be praising his personality. However, to praise what he did we might say, 'The way you've put the tools on the shelf makes the garage look so organized. It's a pleasure to go out there.' or 'Thanks for all the work you did to make the garage look so nice.'"

"Oh, I get it. When you praise a kid's personality, you're kind of labeling him by saying 'you're this' or 'you're that.' It sounds like you are judging him. But when you talk about what he actually did, it's specific, and, to me, that sounds more genuine."

"That's right, when you praise a kid by describing what she did, that creates her 'magic canvas.' She is much more likely to paint that positive picture of herself from your description. This kind of praise would really make a kid feel appreciated too. Also, it says here that *'just praising a kid's personality can make him feel anxious and tense.'*"

"Whoa, that's really interesting." Ted said. "That might just clear up a mystery."

"What do you mean?" I asked curiously.

"Yesterday, when I picked Chris up from Bear Scouts after school, we started talking in the car about the badges he's earned."

"Hasn't he done a super job on those badges?" I said, searching for salad dressing in the refrigerator.

"Absolutely. He has just zipped right through the first six, so I figured he'd be chomping at the bit to get even more. But, when I asked him what he wanted to work on next, he didn't seem to care about earning any more badges. He just said, 'I've done all the badges I can do.'"

"You're kidding!"

"No. I couldn't believe it either. So, I reminded Chris that his Troop Leader, Mr. Johnson, had said, 'Chris, you are so smart. You should easily be able to earn the most badges with hardly any work.'

"I remember when Mr. Johnson said that, Chris seemed so proud and happy."

"I know. That's why I thought it was odd how quiet Chris got, after I reminded him what Mr. Johnson had said. He just sat there, fiddling with the seat belt."

"That is funny, because he's usually so full of energy and talking up a storm when he comes home from Scouts."

"I know. So, I asked him, 'What are you thinking about, Buddy?' You won't believe what he said! He said 'Dad, I'm not as *smart* as Mr. Johnson thinks I am.'"

"Really?" I was astounded. "I can't believe Chris said that."

"I couldn't understand it, either, then. But now, it makes sense. That's exactly what you've just read. Saying things like how *smart* or *wonderful* you are to kids can actually backfire. So, that's why Chris is afraid to work on more badges!"

"I bet you are exactly right, Ted." It became clear to me, too.

Ted went on, "Yeah, all that praise about how smart and wonderful he is has made Chris worried. I think this has put a lot of pressure on him. If Chris fails to earn a certain badge now, to him it would mean he wasn't so smart or wonderful after all. So, for Chris, it's safer to not try, than to try and fail."

Picking up the book again, I read, '*When kids become afraid of losing the label smart or wonderful, they can shut-down. Some kids won't risk even trying if they think their performance reflects their intelligence. The problem is kids can wind up choosing easy tasks, they know they can do, because it's safe and that can limit what they learn.*'"

"Boy is that ever true. People think if you're smart, everything should come easily, which means when you have to work at something, you're not smart."

"Maybe praising Chris's efforts, strategies and accomplishments on the first badges, would encourage him to earn more."

"Now I see how the way we praise kids can affect their thinking. This is what I want to talk about at the meeting tonight. Why don't I write down what I could have said to Chris in the car yesterday?"

"That's great. I'll go upstairs and see if he's awake." When I came back downstairs, Ted was munching on a carrot and staring at a blank computer screen.

He looked up at me sheepishly and said, "Maybe we should do this together. It's harder than it seems. I didn't know where to begin."

"Okay, why don't we use the article to help us get started?" I said picking it up. "It says here that, *'you should picture in your mind exactly what your child has done, and then describe to him in detail what you hear, see, or feel. With this kind of helpful praise, the child should begin to paint a realistic, positive picture of himself.'*"

Ted closed his eyes for a few moments. When he opened them he started typing. Curious, I looked over his shoulder and read what he had typed. "Oh, that's great!"

I said. "I can tell you really pictured Chris working on his First Aid Badge. I can even see him in what you've written."

This is what Ted wrote: Chris, when you practiced the Heimlich Maneuver on me, I really learned something. You helped me remember where to place my hands and what to do if someone begins choking.

"Ted, that is so much more meaningful than just telling Chris he did a great job or how smart he is. What you wrote would let him know he learned how to do the Heimlich, and that he also taught you something. It made me proud just reading it. So, I can only imagine the impact your words would have on Chris. Remember how the child is supposed to paint a positive picture of himself? From what you wrote, Chris certainly would do that."

"Reading this makes me realize I should go up and tell Chris what I wrote," Ted offered.

"I think he'd love it. You'd be recognizing what he learned, and that would help him build the Can-Do Attitude, which is actually the purpose of the Parent Meetings."

Ted looked at me and laughed. "Lisa, I think you just gave *me* helpful praise!"

"Maybe we should call it something different than *praise*," I suggested. "Praise sounds judgmental and can seem insincere and manipulative. I think what we're talking about is more like acknowledging what he's done."

"Or recognizing what he's accomplished," Ted added as he turned back to the computer, "What do you think of calling it Can-Do Recognition?"

"Now I know why I married you. You're not only handsome, you're brilliant!"

"Don't dish out that judgmental praise on me!"

"Oh," I smiled, "Isn't it amazing how easily we fall into that pattern?"

"Yeah. It's going to take some work to break it."

"Well, if it really makes a difference for Chris, I think we need to do it."

"Okay, let's get down to writing those Cliff Notes. In addition to the example, I want to write down the main points. I'm convinced this type of recognition will help kids create the Can-Do Attitude you've been talking about. I can't wait to hear what other people have to say tonight," Ted said as he returned to typing. Here are Ted's Cliff Notes:

Giving Can-Do Recognition

Recognizing a child's strategies, efforts or accomplishments helps build a Can-Do Attitude about life.

1. Picture in your mind exactly what the child has said or done.

2. Describe to him or her in detail what you hear, see, or feel.

3. Let the child know the positive impact of his or her actions.

The child should begin to paint a realistic, positive picture of him or herself.

By the time Ted finished his Cliff notes, the roast was ready. He asked me if I could keep it in the oven for a moment while he ran up to give Chris some Can-Do Recognition.

Chapter 12

Can-Do Recognition

*"So, using the right type of praise
is even more important than we thought."*
- Lisa Davis

I was sound asleep in the den when Ted got home that night. I woke up when he turned the television off. "What time is it?" I asked yawning.

"It's almost ten o'clock," Ted said.

"Wow, it went late tonight."

"Yeah, and everyone wondered where you were. We got so involved talking about how praise affects kids that the time just flew by. I can't believe what I learned."

"Really?" I said, waking up. "Tell me about it."

"Let me look at my notes. Well, in addition to kids becoming anxious or feeling pressured, like you and I talked about, too much of the wrong kind of praise can turn a child into a praise junkie."

"Praise junkie? What a funny term. Does that mean kids can get hooked on praise?" I sat up to hear what he had to say.

"Yeah, kids can become dependent upon constant approval and actually lose their own sense of self-worth. They feel like they've only done a good job if others say so, and that pattern can stay with kids for their whole lives."

"Who would have ever known praise could have that kind of effect on kids?" I couldn't believe the wide role praise played.

"Well, not all types of praise make that happen. Remember that judgmental praise we talked about?" Ted asked.

"You mean saying general things like: 'You're wonderful. You're so smart, or you're brilliant'?"

"Yeah. When those kinds of comments are overused they can create needy children who crave recognition every time they do something."

I told Ted, "So, using the right type of praise is even more important than we thought. Sounds like your Cliff Notes put you on the right track, though."

"Boy they sure did. I'm glad we wrote them. After I heard what everyone had to say about praise, I decided to explain our idea of using Can-Do Recognition instead of praise."

"What did they think about that?"

"At first, the group didn't think praise and recognition were the same. Then I asked them, "What's the purpose of praise?" That opened Pandora's box. Everyone had a different idea. Some people thought it was to get kids to do the right thing. Other people thought it was to make kids feel good about themselves. Then Min asked, 'If praise is for the kids, shouldn't it be meaningful?'"

"That makes sense to me," I said.

"It did to everyone else too. I told them the reason we chose the term *recognition* was because we felt the word praise sounded judgmental and manipulative. We thought if we used *recognition*, it would remind us to praise what Chris had done.

"Maggie agreed, and said, 'I think using the word *recognition* would help us get away from saying comments like 'Great job!' or 'You're so smart!'

"You should have seen Carlos Hernandez. He was up in a flash. I could tell he was pretty upset, when he said, 'Are you trying to tell me I need to stop telling Andy what a great kid he is? I can't believe that! I've worked so hard to get out of the habit of criticizing him. It's taken me months to make sure I praise him enough.'

"Carlos was so worked up I was afraid he might leave. But then Min calmed him down when she said, 'I don't think we want you to stop praising Andy. It's just that how you praise him can make such a huge difference.'

"'What do you mean?' Carlos asked."

I told Ted, "I can't believe how heated the discussion got over praise."

"I know," Ted said. "It was kinda fun. It started to come together when Min explained to Carlos that instead of saying 'That's an awesome job Andy,' he should describe what Andy did. That kind of praise would be more meaningful and helpful for Andy.

"By then, Carlos was starting to relax a little. 'That sounds good,' he told her, 'but I'm going crazy trying to get Andy to pick up his toys in his room after he's done playing. What could I say that would be meaningful about that?'

"You could have heard a pin drop. I could tell that no one really knew how to put our Can-Do Recognition into practice.

"I showed them our Cliff Notes and that got us started. The whole group worked it out together on the flipchart. After about fifteen minutes, this is what we came up with for Carlos."

Ted read from his notes, *"Thanks for working so hard to pick up your toys and putting them in the toy chest, Andy. Your room looks so nice. Now you'll be able to find your toys the next time you want them."*

Ted went on to say, "We all knew Carlos was coming around when he said, 'I like that. If I said that to Andy, I think it would make him feel good about himself. And, he'd know cleaning his room mattered.

"People were so excited about what we had discussed and could see the value of it, everyone wanted to try out Can-Do Recognition. So during the break each one of us tried to give the right kind of recognition to one other person. It was a riot. You wouldn't believe how tongue-tied people got when they first tried it. Pretty soon, though, everyone had the hang of it."

"You're having way too much fun without me," I said.

"Well, you wouldn't have thought that after the break when we had to hammer out our Can-Do Recognition guidelines. It took a while, but this is what we came up with," Ted said as he handed me a piece of paper.

As I looked over what the group had written, I recognized Ted's Cliff Notes, "Ted, they really used your ideas. I'm so proud of you. They would have been totally lost tonight without you."

Can-Do Recognition

Recognizing a child's strategies, efforts, or accomplishments helps build a Can-Do Attitude about life.

How to give Can-Do Recognition

1. Picture in your mind exactly what the child has said or done.

2. Describe to him or her in detail what you hear, see, or feel. (Acknowledging strategy, effort or accomplishment.)
   "You finished your book report (accomplishment). It looks as if you've put a lot of thought into writing it (effort). The way you used colorful words to describe the people and their actions made me feel like I was right there in the story. (strategy)."

3. Let the child know the positive impact or benefit of his or her actions. (optional)
   "What you wrote made me want to read the book, too." (impact) or "You've learned to express your ideas through your book reports (benefit)."

"Oh, it was nothing! But look at the back," he said, turning the paper over. We thought it might be difficult to learn to use Can-Do recognition, so we wrote some examples that people could really use with their kids.

Examples:
- ✓ *Thank you for unloading the dishwasher, Alex. You knew I didn't have time to do that before your grandparents got here. Now we can relax and enjoy our dinner together.*

- ✓ *Andy, you made your room so neat and organized. It's a pleasure to walk in there.*

- ✓ *You've been working on that dance recital all this week, Breanna. That's real dedication. I can tell the difference your practice has made.*

- ✓ *You tied your shoes all by yourself, Sophie!*

"I can just hear the parents giving their kids this kind of recognition. Way to go, Ted!"

As he leaned down to kiss me, Ted said, "Min's going to call us. There's a speaker coming who is an expert on parenting. The whole parent group might go together."

"Gee, Ted, you're really getting into this."

"Yeah, I never knew there was so much to learn about raising kids. Just the little bit I've found out already has made me realize that what I say and do can make a big difference in Chris's life."

I got up from the couch, put my arm through Ted's, and we went up the stairs together.

Chapter 13

Constructive Feedback

"With our constructive feedback we want kids to focus on what happened and how to take the responsibility to do something about it."
- David Garcia

Fortunately, the flu lasted only a few days for Chris. A week after he was back in school, the class was to take the annual Third Grade field trip to the History Museum. I had signed up to go along as a parent volunteer and was looking forward to being with Chris and his classmates.

As Chris and I drove to school the morning of the field trip, we talked about the Bear Scout badge requirement he was working on. It was great to see him excited again about learning a new skill.

As soon as Mr. Garcia took attendance in the classroom, the kids and parents followed him out to the waiting bus. Min, who was also chaperoning that day, and I sat together.

Once we arrived at the museum, Mr. Garcia assigned each parent to a group of kids. A man who was wearing a museum guide badge met us at the door and went over the museum rules with everyone.

We had just entered the first gallery when Mr. Garcia got a phone call from the school. After he hung up, he told us to go on without him. He needed to meet a child who had missed the bus and was arriving late.

As we walked down a long hallway, the kids were talking quietly, pointing at the displays of artifacts we saw at every turn. Then, the guide led us into a room with a huge ceiling. There were dinosaurs everywhere.

When the kids saw replicas of the giant animals, they let out a group "Ahhh!" and suddenly took off running from dinosaur to dinosaur. It was as if the kids had been let loose in Jurassic Park, and they wanted to explore and touch every bit of it. As I began looking around for my group of kids, I suddenly heard an angry voice yelling, "Stop that, right now! Quit doing that! Don't touch anything! Get over here right this minute!"

I looked across the room and saw the guide standing in the doorway. I was embarrassed to see his red face, and I could hear the frustration in his voice, as he tried to get the kids' attention by clapping his hands. When the kids finally quieted down and gathered around the guide, he yelled at them one more time, "You are the worst group I've ever had! You should be ashamed of yourselves for acting like this."

The moment the guide finished his tirade, Mr. Garcia appeared with the missing student by his side. The whole class looked at Mr. Garcia with guilt-ridden faces. I felt embarrassed for the kids' lack of control and wondered how he was going to handle this.

Crossing his arms, the guide looked at Mr. Garcia like it was his fault. Without missing a beat, Mr. Garcia said calmly, "Well kids, it looks like . . ."

All together, the kids finished his sentence by saying, "This is an opportunity for learning."

You should have seen the look on the guide's face and probably on ours, too. Just when we thought we were going to be banished from the museum forever, the atmosphere totally changed.

"Okay, what happened?" Mr. Garcia asked the kids. Several of them slowly raised their hands and told him. When they finished, Mr. Garcia turned to the guide and asked if he wanted to add anything.

Looking very surprised, he said, "No, that's pretty much what happened."

Then Mr. Garcia turned back to the class and asked, "When you act like this, what happens?"

Different kids answered by saying, "The guide gets mad." "We get in trouble." "You get mad at us." "We could get thrown out of the museum."

Mr. Garcia listened carefully and nodded after each comment. When the kids had finished talking, he asked, "What should we do instead?"

I was amazed as I watched the way the kids began responding so thoughtfully by saying, "We should stay in our groups." "We should walk instead of running." "We should follow the Museum rules."

I could tell Mr. Garcia was taking their comments seriously as he nodded in agreement after each statement. Then, he asked, "And, what will happen if we do that?"

Chris looked up at me and raised his hand. When Mr. Garcia called on him he said, "We have fun because we're not getting in trouble."

"What else happens?" Mr. Garcia asked.

Several hands popped up. As Mr. Garcia called on them one at a time, the kids seemed to understand the consequences of their actions. "We get to stay at the museum." "We get to go on more field trips." "People don't get mad at us."

Mr. Garcia turned back to the guide and said, "Do you think we're ready to continue our tour?"

The guide's expression had totally changed. "Mr. Garcia, I believe your class is ready to go on. Let's start with the king of all dinosaurs," he said, leading us over to the Tyrannosaurus Rex that towered over the center of the room.

As we boarded the bus an hour and a half later, I was starving. We were headed to the park where the group was going to stop to eat our sack lunches and enjoy the warm winter day.

When we got to the park, everyone hurried off the bus and ran to find picnic tables. When the kids were finished, I noticed Min waving at me. She was sitting with Mr. Garcia and the other parents at a table near the jungle gym, watching the kids play. When I joined them, I heard Min asking Mr. Garcia about what had happened in the dinosaur gallery.

"I thought you were going to be really mad at the kids for fooling around," she said.

Mr. Garcia laughed, "Yeah, at one time, I might have been. But now, I've found that turning a situation like that into a learning experience is more valuable for all of us."

"Everyone's mood changed when you started asking the kids to think about what they'd done," Min said.

"Well, it's amazing how much kids understand. Sometimes they need a little guidance, but they can usually analyze a situation and come up with some pretty good solutions."

"I was surprised when they knew what to say back to you," Min added.

"The class and I have been working on talking out situations since the beginning of the school year. It's taken a while to get to this point," Mr. Garcia explained. "I'm not the only doing this. In fact, the school staff has taken on a mission to be more constructive in our feedback and criticism."

"Well, I think it's working because instead of cowering with fear, the kids knew they had done something wrong and needed to make a change," another parent said. "Yet, you didn't turn it into a big scene about how bad they had been."

Mr. Garcia nodded. "That's right. We've found that in situations like this, yelling and putting kids down only makes it worse because they get angry and defensive. With our constructive feedback, we want kids to focus on what happened and how to take the responsibility to do something about it."

"It all went so smoothly. Did you have specific questions to ask the kids?" Min wanted to know.

"Sometimes I use questions, and other times I make suggestions. Each staff member has a card with guidelines," he said taking what looked like a business card out of his wallet. He handed the card to Min, and she read it out loud.

Constructive Feedback

When suggesting...	When asking...
1. Describe what happened.	1. Ask what happened.
2. Tell the impact.	2. Ask the impact of what was said or done.
3. Suggest an alternative action.	3. Ask what could be done instead.
4. Explain the benefits of the alternative action(s).	4. Ask the benefits of the new action(s).

"It worked really well when you asked questions. Why would you make suggestions instead?" Min asked.

"Sometimes it's not appropriate to ask questions, when kids won't know the impact of their actions. They might even feel that you're grilling them. When you make a suggestion, and explain the reasoning behind your suggestion, instead of just giving commands, kids are more willing to follow the suggestion."

One of the other parents spoke up. "Can you give us an example?"

"Sure. I'm always giving feedback to kids. Yesterday morning, a child handed in a story she had written. When I sat down with her to edit it, I told her there weren't any periods at the end of her sentences, which made the story hard to read because all her thoughts ran together. I suggested that if she put periods at the end of her sentences, people could read and understand what she wrote."

After hearing Mr. Garcia's explanation, I could understand why it was so important to follow his Constructive Feedback guidelines. I told him, "Knowing the difference it would make in her story, I'll bet that girl wanted to put periods at the end of her sentences."

He smiled and said, "She certainly did."

Min asked Mr. Garcia, "Do you know where I could get some cards like this?"

"Oh, I have lots. Keep that one," he said.

"Thanks. Is it okay with you if I share this with our Can-Do Parent Group? We just talked about using praise, and I think this Constructive Feedback fits right in."

Mr. Garcia responded, "Of course. It would certainly help if parents were giving Constructive Feedback to their kids too."

We all boarded the bus and headed back to school. Fortunately the kids were worn out from their adventure and were quiet all the way home.

Min whispered to me, "Who would have guessed we would learn another parenting skill today?"

Chapter 14

Problem Solving

*"Following these steps with Rachel,
might make it easier for her to talk about the problem.
Nothing is going to get solved,
if she doesn't bring it out in the open."*
          -Maggie Stein

The phone was ringing as I came through the door from work on Friday night. I rushed over to pick it up and was happy to hear Maggie's voice. But before long, I could tell there was something wrong.

"Lisa, do you have a few minutes? I need to talk about a problem I'm having with Rachel," Maggie said in a serious tone.

"You sound upset, are you all right?" I asked her.

"Well…I just don't know where to start. Something happened at school yesterday that has Rachel moping around the house and acting depressed. And she won't tell me what it is."

"That's strange."

"I know. Rachel always talks to me about her problems. Yesterday, as soon as she got home from school, she went straight to her room and closed the door. Later, when I knocked on her door to remind her about basketball practice, she said she had a stomach ache and didn't feel like going. This morning I couldn't get her out of bed, she was still complaining about that same stomach ache. I called into work and told my boss that Rachel was sick and I needed to stay home with her. But at nine o'clock this morning, she didn't seem to be sick at all. Every time I ask her what's wrong, she says 'Nothing Mom' and looks away. I just don't know what to do."

"Have you talked to her teacher?"

"Yeah, I called Mrs. Martin this afternoon. She told me she noticed Rachel got quiet yesterday right after Mrs. Martin assigned the group science fair projects. Tonight, when we were sitting around the family room about an hour ago, I casually asked about the project. Rachel burst into tears and ran into her room, slamming the door."

"Sure sounds like the science fair project is the key, but if she won't talk about, it makes it difficult to help her." I said.

Looking at my watch, I said, "Maggie, I'm sorry, I have to run, it's my turn to drive the carpool, and I have to pick up the kids from soccer practice in ten minutes. Can we talk later tonight?"

"Of course. I'm so glad you were home. Just talking about it has helped me. I'll be here all evening. Call me when you have time."

I kept thinking about Maggie's dilemma, and after dinner, when Ted and I were cleaning up the kitchen, he said to me, "You seem to have something on your mind. You've been so quiet tonight. Is everything okay?"

"Well, Maggie called me this afternoon. She's having quite a time with Rachel. I need to call her back, but I'm dreading it because I don't know how to help her," I admitted.

"So, what's going on?" Ted asked.

I told Ted about Maggie's phone call. He listened intently and when I finished, he looked at me and said, "You know, it sounds like Rachel has given up and doesn't think she can solve her problem, whatever it is. Her self efficacy level must be low."

"Her what? Ted, are you trying to impress me with your *hifalutin* words?"

He laughed. "Well, I can tell you're impressed. Actually, it's a term we learned during our corporate training program on problem solving. It has to do with how a person feels about his own ability. If you feel you have the power to make something happen, you will take action. If you don't think you have any power, you won't even try to do it."

"That sounds like what Rachel is doing by staying home from school and refusing to tell Maggie what's going on."

"Exactly. When people feel helpless, they may clam up because don't know what to do. She might even be embarrassed."

"So, how could a corporate training program help a little girl in elementary school?"

"Well, the problem solving process is a tool that anybody could use, no matter what age. The steps are the same, it's just the problems that become more complicated as we get older."

"A tool? What do mean?"

"Say you wanted to hang a picture, and had this big old nail, but didn't have any tools in the house. What would you do?"

"That's simple. I'd wait until you got home from work."

Ted laughed, "But if you had a hammer available, you could easily pound the nail right into the wall."

"Yeah, if I had the hammer, I could hang the picture myself."

"Just like I always say . . ."

"When you have the right tool, everything is easier!" Ted and I said at the same time. Laughing, we high-fived over the kitchen table.

Ted continued to explain, "A problem solving process is a tool, just like a hammer. The hammer can be there, but you have to be the one to pick it up and use it."

"Do you think if Maggie and Rachel use this tool you're talking about that it could help Rachel open up and talk to her mom?"

"Yeah, I do. From what I've seen at work, when this process or tool is used, it has helped take the emotion out of problem solving. Working through the problem solving steps teaches people that they have more options for solving their problems." As I listened to Ted, I thought what he said made sense, and I was grateful for his concern.

I told him, "Right now, I think Maggie would be willing to try anything, but you'd have to be the one to explain this to her. Why don't I call her and ask her to come over? Besides, this sounds like something we should include in our Can-Do Attitude toolbox."

Ted went upstairs to check on Chris who was doing his homework in his room, while I called Maggie.

"I'll be right over," she said as the phone clicked.

When I let Maggie in, she gave me a hug. "Lisa, I truly appreciate your help," she said.

"It was really Ted who thought of a way you might be able to work through this problem with Rachel."

Just then, Ted came down the stairs and offered Maggie a cup of coffee, as we all went into the kitchen together.

When we were seated around the table Ted, explained. "When Lisa told me what was going on with Rachel, it reminded me of a problem solving process we've been learning to use at work. I've really been surprised at how following a structured process helps put the focus on the problem, not on the people involved. When we've done this at work, we've come up with some amazing solutions."

"Well, I don't know how we're going to come up with any workable solutions until Rachel tells me what the problem is." I could hear the frustration in Maggie's voice.

"That's the beauty of this process. Going through the steps helps people open up and creates an opportunity for thoughtful discussion about the problem. That way, people aren't just reacting automatically to the problem and doing the first thing that pops into their heads," Ted explained.

"I'm not sure I understand how this relates to Rachel," Maggie said.

"Let me tell you about when we used this method at work recently. Two people in my department, I'll call them Keisha and Hal, had to have time off at the same time next month. And they both had very legitimate reasons. Keisha is going to be a bridesmaid in an out-of-town family wedding, and Hal is scheduled for back surgery. Unfortunately, it's the only week Hal's doctor is available. It's a real problem because this is our busy time of year, and there's no way we can afford to have them both gone at the same time."

"That's definitely a problem," Maggie said. "It's a no-win situation."

"No kidding! At first, I thought maybe I'd just take that week off too and go on a cruise," Ted said with a grin.

"You're not going without me," I added.

Ted smiled, "Then, as I was sitting in my office, trying to figure out what to do, I saw the bright blue training notebook for the Problem Solving course glaring at me from the pile of books on my desk. I picked it up and said to myself – what do I have to lose? Let's try this on a real problem."

"What happened?" Maggie asked.

"Well, I called Keisha and Hal to ask them if they would be willing to try this new problem solving process on our vacation time dilemma. After all, they had both taken the training class, too. Both of them were willing to take a stab at it."

Ted picked up his briefcase and got out the bright blue notebook.

"Aha, the book with all the answers," I couldn't help saying.

"Not exactly. We are the ones who have to come up with the answers. This just guides us through the process." We watched Ted flip through the notebook until he found the page he wanted. Taking it out, he laid it on the table in front of Maggie and me. At the top of the page it said, *Problem Solving Steps.*

Picking up the page, Maggie said, "Well, this doesn't look too complicated.

"It's not when you follow the steps in order," Ted said. "Go ahead, Maggie, and read the steps to us."

Maggie read:

1. Describe what's happening, without blaming.
2. Brainstorm all the potential resulting problems.
3. Decide on the most important problem.
4. Brainstorm options for solving the problem.
5. Choose a solution and carry it out.
6. Evaluate result - did it work or not?"

"Gee, it doesn't sound complicated, but I think going through six steps would take a long time," I said.

"Well, it did take time and thought but it was worth it because Keisha and Hal walked out of the conference room still talking to each other," Ted said with a grin. "Man, was I ever relieved. I can laugh about it now, but it sure wasn't funny at the time."

"Really." Maggie said. "Tell us what you decided to do."

"Well, it was a joint decision. First, we all sat around a table in the conference room and talked about the problem – both needing the same week off and why. As they each explained their reasons, they seemed to have an understanding of the other person's needs. It appeared that they became more dedicated to finding a solution that would work for both of them."

"Awwwww . . . " Maggie and I said at the same time.

Looking over his glasses at us, Ted cleared his throat. "For step number two, we brainstormed, by writing down all the problems we could have if two people were gone during the busy time of year. We came up with seven problems. Once, we had them written down and could look at them on paper, the most important problem was like a flashing red light."

"I'm dying to know what that was," I said.

"Well, we could see that there were two reports that absolutely have to be finished that week. Everything else could be done in advance, or wait a week, or could be done by somebody else."

"So, the fourth step, according to your sheet, says to brainstorm options," Maggie said.

"We had fun working on that one. In fact, we came up with about twenty options to solve the problem. I'll admit some of them were wild and crazy, but when brainstorming, *all* ideas are accepted because some of the last ones might be the best.

"And, you don't want to shut anyone down by criticizing their ideas," Maggie jumped in.

"You're right," Ted agreed.

"I'd like to hear some of those wild and crazy ones," I said laughing.

"Well, our last idea was to let Hal recuperate from his surgery in the guest room, at our house, with you waiting on him," Ted said looking at me.

I laughed, "I know that's not the one you chose. So what did you decide to do?"

"Before we made a decision, we listed the factors involved because that would determine which ideas were workable. For example, Hal and Keisha are the only ones who know how to do the reports. Also, we don't have room in the budget to pay overtime. But then we figured out that all the information needed for the reports would be available late on the Friday their vacations began."

Maggie jumped up and said, "Maybe they could stay late on Friday and do the reports."

"See how easy it is to get involved?" Ted said laughing, as Maggie sat back down with an embarrassed look on her face. "But you're warm. Keisha and Hal are both coming into work, on the Saturday their vacations begin. Working together, they are going to get the reports out that day."

"Well, that sounds pretty simple," I said.

"It does now, but if I had asked them to do this, they probably would have resented working on their own time. But, when we worked it out together, it became a labor of love."

This time, Maggie and I both groaned at the same time. "Oh, Ted," I said as Maggie laughed.

"That's only five steps," I said looking at the sheet.

"Yeah, once we've carried out the plan, the three of us will sit down together and evaluate how it worked. That's step six. If it doesn't work, we'll talk about what we could have done differently." Ted sounded so proud of the way it had all worked out.

"It seems to me the most important part of problem solving is that it gets the focus off the person, and onto the problem." Maggie said. "Following these steps with Rachel, might make it easier for her to talk about the problem. Nothing is going to get solved, if she doesn't bring it out in the open."

Ted nodded. "I agree. I think this process might help you and Rachel work through whatever is bugging her."

"I hope so. It couldn't hurt to try. Do you have an extra copy of those steps, Ted?" Maggie asked.

"I have a whole tablet of worksheets. Here take a few," Ted said as he tore off several sheets and handed them to her.

"I don't know what I'd do if I didn't have the two of you next door," Maggie said as she looked at the sheets. "You can bet I'll let you know how it all comes out."

    I walked Maggie to the door, and gave her a hug. As I watched her go down our steps and across the yard, I knew how concerned she was about Rachel. It seemed like problems were always coming up when raising kids. Being a parent is such a huge responsibility, I was glad to know there were some proven tools and support systems out there to help us get through it.

Chapter 15

Can-Do Problem Solving

"That's right, just the facts, Ma'am."
-Ted Davis

By Sunday, I couldn't stand the suspense any longer. I decided to call Maggie right after lunch to find out what had happened.

"Hi Lisa, I'm glad you called," Maggie said, sounding like her old self again. "You're going to be surprised when you find out what was bugging Rachel."

"Tell me," I said.

"First, getting into the Problem Solving Process wasn't quite as easy as it sounded when Ted was explained it the other night. I intended to talk to Rachel Saturday morning after she finished her breakfast."

"Sounds like a plan," I said.

"Yeah, but it didn't exactly work that way. When Rachel walked into the kitchen, she said, 'Hi Mom,' grabbed some toast and juice and plopped herself in front of the television, before I could say a word."

I laughed, thinking about how Chris is glued to his favorite cartoons every Saturday morning.

"I thought about asking her to turn off the TV. But her mood seemed better, so I didn't want to spoil the moment, if you know what I mean," Maggie went on. "Besides, I was a little tongue tied about how I was going to tell her that I wanted to try using a problem solving worksheet with her."

"I know, hearing about it is one thing, but actually doing it is another."

"Yeah, but I knew Rachel and I absolutely had to discuss her problem. So, I figured a good time to talk would be coming home from the dentist later that morning. The two of us would be alone in the car without any distractions."

"That sounds perfect. So?"

"Right after we left the dentist's office, Rachel asked if we could stop at the mall. I looked at her and said, 'Well, you must be feeling a lot better today.' She said, 'Yeah, I am.' Then I realized it was Saturday and she was probably relieved that school wasn't an issue over the weekend. I thought about just letting it go, but I knew we had to deal with the situation, and this was the perfect chance."

"How did you get started?" I asked.

"There didn't seem to be a right time, so I decided to bite the bullet and just start. When we got to the freeway, I said to Rachel, 'Look sweetheart, you know you have to go back to school on Monday. There's no question about that. However, I know something has been bothering you, and you have some choices to make.' I could tell I was on the right track when she nodded her head."

"It sounds like she was ready to tell you what was bothering her."

"That's what I read in her face, too. So, I said, 'Rachel, you can go back to school on Monday and face whatever happened on your own. Or, we can talk about it together and try to figure out how to solve whatever problem you have. I was over at Ted and Lisa's last night, and Ted gave me a worksheet that might help us work through this problem.'"

"What did she say?"

"She sounded pretty annoyed and asked me if I had told you she'd been home from school. Of course, I told her the truth. I explained that since you are my best friend and I was so worried about her, I had to talk to someone. She seemed okay with that. Rachel really likes you and Ted."

"That's good. I'm glad she could understand."

"Then I told her a little bit about the problem solving process Ted had shown us. I explained that everybody has problems, and it's important to use your energy to work problems out instead of spending energy worrying about them. When I looked over at her, I saw a tear falling down her face."

"Oh, you must have felt awful."

"I did, but I knew she needed help, and I was relieved Rachel was finally letting me in. I asked her if she would like to have me help her work through her problem. All of a sudden, it was as if a dam had burst. The words started spilling out of her mouth. Rachel told me everything that happened at school Thursday. I tried to listen without making any judgments or comments."

"You have me on pins and needles. What could be so devastating that a girl who loves school faked being sick to stay home?"

"Well, it was a problem with two of her friends. For some reason, they got mad at Rachel after the three of them started working together on the science fair project Thursday morning. The two girls ignored Rachel the rest of the day and even got some of the other girls in class to snub her, too."

"You're kidding."

"No. In fact, when Rachel sat down at the lunch table next to them, they got up and moved to a different table, leaving her sitting there all by herself. She felt so hurt, she didn't know what to do. When she went back to the classroom, she told Mrs. Martin she had an upset stomach and asked if she could go to the nurse. Since Rachel didn't have a temperature, the nurse didn't call me, but she let Rachel rest in her office the rest of the afternoon."

"Wow! No wonder she didn't want to go to school the next day. I sure wouldn't want to."

"Who would? What surprised me was that the two girls who were assigned to do the project with Rachel used to be her best friends. At first I was so mad at them for doing that to her, I wanted to call their parents and have a meeting with the principal first thing Monday morning. I even thought about driving over to their houses and confronting the girls right then."

"Kids can be mean."

"But, by the time we got home from the dentist, I had calmed down a little and began to wonder what might have happened that caused the girls to treat Rachel that way. That's when I decided that using the Problem Solving Process might really be helpful. We needed to take the emotion out, so we could get to the heart of the problem."

"Did it work?"

"You won't believe it, but Rachel and the other two girls are getting together this afternoon to work on the project."

"No way!"

"Yeah. Rachel and I have to leave in a few minutes."

"Oh no! You can't leave me hanging. I'm dying to know how you worked this out."

"I can't wait to tell you either, but I have to run. Are you going to be home later this afternoon? I'd love to come over and show you the worksheet we used. I thought Ted might like to see it, too, because Rachel and I made a few changes in the wording to make it kid-friendly."

"Great. How about somewhere between 4:00 and 5:00? We'll both be home then. I'm so glad things are working out, and Ted will be, too."

"Okay. See you later," Maggie said as she hung up the phone.

Hearing the bounce of a basketball, I wandered outside to the driveway where Ted and Chris were shooting baskets together. I laughed as I saw Ted attempt a basket from halfway across the driveway. When the ball completely missed the basket and hit the pavement, Chris grabbed it. Dribbling the ball over to where Ted had been standing, Chris threw the ball up across the driveway. The three of us watched it swoosh right through the middle of the hoop. Ted fell on the ground in defeat. Chris went over to his dad and gave him the ball. "Let's play one more game, Dad."

Ted got up. Patting Chris on his back, he said, "You're on, Buddy." Ted smiled when he saw me watching. He called out, "Have you talked to Maggie?"

I knew he was eager to know what had happened with Rachel, too. "I just called her," I said. "She and Rachel used your worksheet, and she wants to come over this afternoon to show us what they came up with. From what she said, it sure sounds like it helped them out."

"I'm glad to hear that," Ted said as made a lay-up and threw Chris the ball.

"Nice shot, Dad," Chris said as he followed with a lay-up of his own. When I turned around and went back inside, I smiled as I heard the thump of the basketball on the concrete.

It was around ten to five when our doorbell rang that afternoon. I saw Maggie standing there, and I could tell by the expression on her face that things had gone well with the girls. "Ted, Maggie's here," I called out as the two of us walked toward the kitchen.

When the three of us were seated around the kitchen table once again, Maggie said, "I can't believe how helpful the problem solving process was. The questions helped us focus on the facts and kept us on track. Thanks, Ted."

"Aw shucks, it was nothing, Ma'am," Ted said doing his best cowboy impression.

Maggie and I rolled our eyes, and laughed.

"I can't believe the three girls actually got together today to work on the school project," I said. "How did you ever pull that off?"

"Well, the first breakthrough came when Rachel opened up. After she finished talking, she admitted there had been this huge lump in her throat since Thursday. She said it went away as soon as she told me the whole story. Oh, by the way, Rachel said it was okay if I share this with you," Maggie said.

"That was nice of her," I thought it was great the way Maggie respected Rachel's privacy.

Maggie smoothed out the problem solving worksheet on the table. "The second breakthrough came when we were working on this. It might look pretty easy now that it's all filled out, but let me tell you, at times it was painful for both of us. When Rachel and I started talking about what happened at school, she got upset all over again and started crying. After talking for a few minutes, we started over and actually followed the instructions. We tried to just write down the facts, without blaming or criticizing anybody for anything."

"That's right, just the facts, Ma'am," Ted added.

Maggie shook her head, "Ted, you are too much. But, you're right. Sticking to the facts took a lot of the emotion out, and by the time we came up with our solution, Rachel had calmed down and actually realized that there was something *she* could do and that she didn't need to be a victim of the circumstances. That was her third breakthrough, and it gave her a surge of energy. She began to think of different ways to solve the problem.

"You know, Ted, I like what you said about *the facts*," Maggie said as she reached over and picked up a pen lying on our computer desk. She crossed out the first question on the worksheet. Above it she wrote "Just the Facts." Then she put the worksheet on the table so it was right in front of us. Ted and I both read it over to ourselves.

PROBLEM SOLVING PROCESS (PSP)
Just the facts

1. <u>What happened?</u> (Without criticism or blame)

    When Jasmine, Hannah and I were working on the science fair project together, they called me bossy and said I was a know-it-all. I asked Mrs. Martin if I could work with another group. She said no, we had to work together. The girls ignored me the rest of the day and when I sat next to them at lunch, they got up and moved to another table.

2. <u>What caused this to happen?</u>

    I think they got mad when I wanted to do my science fair project idea instead of theirs. My idea was the best, but they wouldn't listen to me. Then, they took sides against me and called me bossy and stopped talking to me. Maybe I was a little bossy, but I knew I was right.

3. <u>What are possible options?</u>
    1. *Pretend I'm sick until the science fair is over.*
    2. *Ask the Mrs. Martin to help us work it out.*
    3. *Ignore the girls and act like they don't bother me.*
    4. *Act nice, try not to be so bossy when I see them again.*
    5. *Call and talk out the problem with the girls*

4. <u>What will affect the solution?</u>
    1. *I have to go to school.*
    2. *It's a group project that I <u>have</u> to do with Jasmine and Hannah.*
    3. *We need to get along, even if we aren't best friends.*

5. <u>What's the best solution?</u> *(Is it possible and appropriate?)*

    Make the effort to get along with Jasmine and Hannah. Call them and talk the problem out. Offer to use everybody's ideas equally.

6. <u>Carry it out and evaluate results.</u>

[*]"Wow! She stayed home from school because some girls were mean to her," Ted said.

"Children focus on what's happening *right now* in their lives. When the girls ignored her, Rachel felt like an outcast and felt helpless to do anything about it," I explained. "Imagine how she must have felt when those girls got up and left her sitting all alone at the lunch table."

"When Rachel told me that, I was devastated," Maggie said. "But, it was exciting when Rachel discovered she had more control over the problem than she thought she did. This gave her the confidence to call the girls. She knew she had a back-up plan. If the first one didn't work out, she knew she could try some of the other options she had come up with."

"By George, I think she's got it!" Ted piped up.

"More than you know." Maggie smiled as she said, "In fact, when we were coming home from Jasmine's, I mentioned that I needed to get the car into the shop but I didn't know how I was going to do it. This week I have so many things going on, I just need to have the car. Well, Rachel jumped in and said, 'Mom, don't you think you should use Ted's worksheet for your problem?'"

---

[*] Blank form for the Problem Solving Process can be found in the Appendix.

I laughed picturing Maggie's face at that comment.

"You know, it really worked. Rachel and I figured out some other options for the car, but I want you to hear how Rachel's solution worked out. Listen to this," Maggie said as she started reading out loud.

Step 6 – Evaluation

It was hard for me to call the girls. I talked to my Mom and she helped me write down what I was going to say on the phone. I was really happy to hear the girls say they had been worried about me when I wasn't in school Friday. They said they were sorry for being mean, and I said I was sorry for being bossy. Jasmine invited Hannah and me to come over Sunday afternoon to work on the project. (Yea!)

I was nervous about meeting with the girls. Once we got started, everything was okay. We voted and chose Jasmine's idea for our project. We decided to take turns being the leader when we work together. Sometimes I had to stop myself from being bossy.

I was happy when Jasmine and Hannah liked some of my ideas. I'm proud of myself for working it out. I'm really glad my Mom helped me. I can't wait to go to school tomorrow.

<u>Things for me to work on</u>: Not being so bossy. Listening when my friends are talking. Use my friends' ideas too.

Ted hit the table when Maggie finished reading. "Wow! When I gave the problem solving process to you, I figured it would be helpful. But your using it turned out way better than I expected!"

"Yeah and I can't believe the change that came over all the girls," I said.

"It was just as Ted explained," Maggie said. "Using the process allowed Rachel to take the emotion out and work realistically and logically on her problem. It amazed me, too."

"And this part *Things I can work on,*" Ted said pointing at the bottom of the Evaluation, "is a great addition to the process. In fact, I'm going to add that to the worksheet I use."

"That was Rachel's idea. She wrote those down as reminders to herself." Looking at the kitchen clock Maggie said, "Oh, I've got to run. I can't tell you how much I appreciate both of you for helping us through this. I was going bananas!"

Later that night, when I was turning off the lights on my way up the stairs, I reminded myself to call Min the next day. I wanted to make sure Ted's Problem Solving Worksheet was on the agenda for the next Parent

Group meeting. It was another essential element, I felt, for helping kids build a Can-Do Attitude.

Chapter 16

The Goal Trap

"Learning is a way of life. We have tons of opportunities to teach kids how important learning is every single day."
— Dr. Richard Chambers

"Chris," I called upstairs, "your grandmother is here." Knowing he would be down in a flash to greet her, I went into the kitchen to turn off the buzzing oven timer.

We were always glad when my mother could stay with Chris while Ted and I went out. Many times we had come home to find a "creation" the two of them had whipped up with stuff they found around our house. Looking at the kitchen door, I saw one of my favorites, a large rock Mom and Chris had painted to look like a real slice of watermelon. It was a perfect doorstop and always made me smile when I saw it.

I heard the front door slam as Chris ran out to meet his grandmother, and it wasn't long until the two of them came into the kitchen with Bailey at their heels. Chris was talking excitedly. "Grandma, wait until you see all the books I've read! I've got more Heavenly Tickets than anybody in my class."

"That's great, honey, but what's a Heavenly Ticket?" my mother asked. Then she looked over at me and asked, "And what's that heavenly smell?"

"It's your lasagna recipe, Mom. So, you know it will be delicious," I said taking it out of the oven.

She laughed and then looked back at Chris.

He went on, "Every time I read 10 books, I get a ticket for a free hamburger at Hamburger Heaven, and I have 3 of them already."

"Wow, that's 30 books, Chris. How long have you been doing this?" I could tell my mother was impressed.

"This whole month, and this is the last week," Chris explained, holding up some books. "If I finish these three books tonight, I'll get another Heavenly Ticket tomorrow."

"Hmmm. Looks like we won't be making anything tonight. You've already got your work cut out for you," my mother said as she smiled at Chris and gave him a hug.

Chris set the books down on the kitchen table. "I'll be right back. I'm gonna go get my tickets so I can show them to you, Grandma," Chris said, tearing up the stairs.

I saw my mother pick up and leaf through one of the books Chris had just set down. "Gee, Lisa, this looks awfully easy for him," she sounded concerned.

"You're probably right," I said as I opened the cupboard and took out the dinner plates. "I think he read that book in second grade. But it's all right because according to the rules it just has to be a book he hasn't read *this* year. What's great is ever since Hamburger Heaven started this reading incentive program, Chris has been bringing home library books by the dozen."

"Well, no wonder he's read so many so quickly," my mother said, picking up the other two books. "These all look a little easy for him." She put Chris's books on our computer desk and took placemats out of a drawer.

Just then, Chris ran back in waving his Heavenly Tickets. "When I get one more, I can take us all out to eat," he said proudly to my mother.

"I'd love to go to Hamburger Heaven with you. It was my favorite place to eat when I was in high school. In fact, it was the first place I went with your grandfather on a date," my mother said. "By the way, Chris, did you finish that Harry Potter book I gave you for your birthday?"

"Nah. That's way too long. I can read twenty books in the time it takes to read a Harry Potter book! I'd never get any Heavenly Tickets reading that," Chris said as he got out the silverware and started helping my mother set the table.

I noticed she had a funny look on her face, and I could tell something was on her mind. Curious, I decided to ask her about it when Ted and I got home later that night.

Just then, Ted came into the room sniffing. "Mmmmm. Smells like my favorite Italian restaurant in here." Swooping my mother off her feet, he gave her a kiss on the cheek. "Thanks for staying with Chris, Linda, so I can take my favorite gal out on the town."

"Well, I wouldn't exactly call tonight's meeting 'out on the town,'" I said looking at Ted. Turning to my mother I explained, "You know, our parenting group that we go to? Well, instead of meeting at someone's house this month, we're all going to hear a parenting expert the school district brought in. It's at the high school and we're going to talk about it at the next meeting."

When the dinner dishes were finished, and Ted and I were ready to leave, I gave my mother a hug. "We shouldn't be too late," I said, noticing Chris was already sitting on the couch reading with Bailey beside him.

A half hour later, we were comfortably settled in our seats at the high school auditorium. I waved across the aisle when I saw Min and Maggie, sitting next to each other.

The auditorium lights dimmed and everyone quieted down. I recognized the school board president as she walked up to the podium to introduce the speaker, Dr. Richard Chambers. Hearing his background made me eager to listen to what this nationally known educational psychologist and parent had to say.

Dr. Chambers walked to the center of the stage, stopped, and turned to the audience. Holding the microphone in front of his mouth, he asked, "How many of you give your kids rewards like money, gold stars, or some sort of prize when they get good grades?"

A sea of hands fluttered across the crowded auditorium. I noticed Carlos, nodding his head in the next row as he held his hand high.

No one was prepared for what Dr. Chambers said next. Slowly and deliberately he continued, "When you give children rewards for performance, you can shut the door on their learning." There was a hush in the room as the hands went down. He had our attention now.

"I know this comes as a shock to most of you because giving rewards for performance has become the way we do things," the speaker said.

Ted leaned over and whispered to me, "I'm outta here. This guy's a quack."

I patted Ted's knee. "Give him a chance, honey," I whispered back. "This guy's nationally known."

"Just because he's famous, doesn't mean he knows what he's talking about," Ted said.

"I know, but let's at least hear what he has to say." I gave Ted my best smile as he sat back in his seat.

Dr. Chambers went on. "Money for grades, gold stars on charts, or prizes can cause kids to focus on the prize, instead of the learning."

There was a low murmur in the crowd, and I could see a man wearing a dark green shirt frantically waving his hand.

When Dr. Chambers called on him, the man said, "You've got to be kidding. If I don't give my son $20 for every A and $10 for a B, he'd never be on the honor roll." As the man sat down, I saw other parents shaking their heads in agreement with what he had just said.

Looking out at the audience, Dr. Chambers went on, "Just because kids get good grades, it doesn't mean they are learning or working to their potential. When you give kids rewards for grades or results, you teach them to only care about the reward. You know you've done this when kids ask you 'What do I get for doing this?'"

"I can't believe what you're saying. That's exactly what my son said to me last week," the man in the green shirt said. "When I told him it was his job to take out the trash, he asked me, 'What do I get for it?'"

As his words sank in, my mother's face flashed in front of me. Now, I knew what her look had been about. Chris was reading easy books just because of what he could get for it—the Heavenly Tickets—and to be the one who read the most books in his class. *He wasn't learning anything new!*

Dr. Chambers brought me back to the present when he asked, "How many of you have ever crammed for a test?" Hands went up all around us. Ted looked over at me. Both of us had our hands up, too.

"And, how many of you remembered what you crammed into your brain when the test was over?" Dr. Chambers asked next. Almost every hand went down.

Dr. Chambers continued, "That's because you were *only* occupied with the end result – getting a good grade or passing the test. That's called a Performance Goal. And, when we give kids rewards *only* for their performance, we teach them the result is the *only* thing that counts."

The man in the green shirt was on his feet again. "But grades are important!" he blurted out. "My son won't get into a good school, if he doesn't get good grades."

Dr. Chambers nodded. "You are absolutely right. Grades are very important and critical and so are Performance Goals."

Then he went on to explain, "Challenging Performance Goals like getting good grades, winning a game or even going to the moon energize people, give them purpose and keep them on track. When someone is committed to an ambitious goal, it motivates her to learn new skills and go beyond what she's ever done before.

"I'm sure everyone here has conquered a challenging goal at some time in life. Think about how motivated you were at that time. And that's a good thing. It's when we *over emphasize* Performance Goals that we create problems."

Walking back to the podium, he put a chart up on the screen. "This chart shows what happens when kids are *only* focused on Performance Goals."

Over Emphasizing Performance Goals *can cause children to:*
- Do only what is required
- Have more anxiety about doing it right
- Learn superficially
- Play it safe to look smart or competent
- Feel put down by their mistakes
- Devalue what's being rewarded
- Sometimes cheat to finish or win
- Blame failure on others or circumstances
- Not ask for help when they need it because they are afraid they will look "stupid"

The man in the green shirt was up again. "Okay, I can see your point, but how do we change our kids' focus so the performance isn't over emphasized?"

"This is where our job as adults comes in. We can help kids learn to put the proper balance between Performance Goals and Learning Goals. When kids combine the two goals—performance and learning, they get enthused and excited about what they are learning."

Dr. Chambers directed his attention to the man in the green shirt. "In fact, your son will get *better* grades, if he is interested in what he is learning. When the goal is to learn, the reward becomes the learning itself." Dr. Chambers walked back to the podium, "This is what happens when a child focuses on learning goals," he said as another chart appeared on the screen.

Focusing on Learning Goals

Puts the attention on personal development and can cause children to:

- Be energized about mastering new skills and information
- Have less anxiety in general
- Have a deeper understanding and enjoy what they are learning
- Be willing to explore and try new ways
- See stumbling blocks as enjoyable challenges
- Keep going when they come to obstacles
- Ask for help when needed
- See mistakes as a valuable way to learn
- Be motivated to keep learning

A woman sitting in front of me raised her hand. Dr. Chambers pointed to her, and she asked, "That all sounds great, but how do I get my daughter to give up expecting rewards for good grades, weekly chores, and for just being good?"

Dr. Chambers chuckled at this and said, "VERY SLOWLY. Once you've promised kids rewards, you can't just take them away. You've created a bargain with your child, and if you change that all of a sudden, you could lose her trust. But, what you can do is gradually start to shift her attention away from rewards and toward learning goals."

It seemed like the whole audience let out a sigh of relief at the same time.

Hands shot up all over the room. Dr. Chambers motioned to a woman with red hair. She asked, "So what's the magic formula for getting my kids to focus on learning?"

"There is no magic formula," Dr. Chambers said. "Learning is a way of life. We have tons of opportunities to teach kids how important learning is every single day."

"What do you mean?" the woman asked.

"Just the way you ask a child about her day can make the difference in how much she learns. When the first words out of your mouth are 'What grade did you get?' You're telling a child it's *only* the grade that's important."

The woman looked confused. "You said grades are important, and I do need to know how my daughter's doing. So, what else could I say?"

"If you ask, 'What did you *learn* today?, you're letting her know *learning* is what's important. Try asking your child, 'What did you learn today' five times for every 'How did you do?' And then, listen and talk to her about what she tells you. You do that for a month and come back and tell me how she's doing. I guarantee she will be doing better in school and enjoying it more."

I knew Ted had been won over when he whispered to me, "You know, I could do that with Chris."

Dr. Chambers went on, "And, how about those works of art your child brings home? How often do you gush over them and say, 'That's beautiful'? I know there is nothing that will ever stop you, especially those grandparents out there, from telling kids how fabulous, fantastic, and wonderful they are."

The audience laughed at this.

"But, if we want to encourage a child to develop a love of learning, we can ask him questions like, 'Why did you choose these colors?' 'Tell me about your project,' or 'What were you thinking when you wrote this story?' Those are just a few ways to help a child want to go on learning." Dr. Chambers said as he stepped back to the podium.

Min raised her hand. "I just wrote down those questions to ask my kids, and I noticed you never said to say '*I* like this or that.' Was that on purpose?"

Dr. Chambers smiled. "Yes, it was. When you tell a child '*I liked your picture*', you are focusing the child on your approval. But, when you ask him to talk about what he created, it becomes about what he did."

"That makes a big difference in the message I could be giving my kids," Min said.

A man in the front row stood up next. "This all makes lots of sense to me, but I don't want to give up giving rewards to my kids completely. We enjoy making a big deal when they do something wonderful," he said.

I saw other parents nodding their heads, and saying "me too," as I looked around the crowd.

Dr. Chambers said, "Of course you should celebrate. It's what you reward and celebrate with your kids that makes the difference. Instead of rewarding the A's, consider rewarding the learning. For example, celebrate when your child learns the multiplication tables, how to ride a bike, or how to play the trumpet. You could celebrate progress or improvement, for instance, when your child moves to the next level on the piano, math or reading."

I was surprised to see Ted was waving his hand. Dr. Chambers called on him. "What you're saying is to try to reward what kids learn instead of the results, right?" Ted asked.

"That is what I'm saying. That will help kids shift their focus from just performance to being interested and motivated to learn. It's okay to celebrate performance, from time to time. Just make sure that's not the main focus."

When Dr. Chambers finished, everyone clapped. Thinking about his first comment and the shock it created, I never would have thought it possible. At the end, though, the crowd seemed to be upbeat and talking to each other. I heard positive comments like—"I'm so glad I came" and "I could really do this" which was exactly the way I felt, too.

Arriving home, we found my mother curled up on the couch. Her magazine was on the floor where it must have dropped when she fell asleep. She was tired when we woke her up, but wouldn't leave until she'd heard all about our evening.

When we explained what Dr. Chambers said about rewards and prizes, she said "I knew something wasn't right about Chris reading all those easy books."

Ted, Bailey, and I walked Mom out to her car. As she drove down the street, I said to Ted, "I know we can't do anything about Chris's performance goal to get one more Heavenly Ticket. But when the reading program is over this Friday, I'm determined to work on focusing his attention on reading some books that truly challenge him."

Ted laughed, holding Bailey's leash. "Sounds like you were listening tonight, honey. Learning Goals here we come!"

Chapter 17

Can-Do Goals

"Being responsible is a big part of a Can-Do Attitude."
-Carlos Hernandez

It was a warm April evening, so Ted and I decided to walk the three blocks to Carlos's house for the Can-Do Parent Meeting. I insisted we take along an umbrella, even though Ted thought I was crazy.

As we were walking, the smell of jasmine surrounded us. "I just love spring, when everything is so fresh and green," I said, glad to be out in the night air. Just then, Ted reached down to pet the neighbor's calico cat that had been following us.

The cat flopped down on the sidewalk, content to stay there as we walked on. Ted looked over at me and said, "I still can't believe you brought that umbrella on a night as beautiful as this."

"You never know at this time of year. Better safe than sorry," I said poking him gently with the umbrella.

When we got to Carlos's house, a woman with light brown hair opened the door. I offered her my hand, "You must be Sandy, Carlos's wife. I'm Lisa Davis, and this is my husband, Ted."

Sandy smiled as we shook hands. "Yes, I'm so glad to meet you, Lisa and Ted. It's heaven not being on the night shift at the hospital anymore so I can get to know everyone Carlos has talked about. He comes home from these meetings excited to tell me what you've been reading and discussing. And, I've seen a real change in Carlos and Andy's relationship. Carlos is much more patient with our son."

I nodded my head, "These meetings have made a difference in how we relate to our son, Chris, too. Ted and I couldn't be happier with the changes in all of us," I told her. Then, I asked Sandy if it was alright to leave my umbrella by the front door. She took it and set it next to several others propped up against the wall.

We followed Sandy into the living room, and I could see there was a big crowd, even a few new faces. The buzz of excited chatter filled the room.

Ted and I found two empty folding chairs just as Carlos was calling the meeting to order. After everyone introduced themselves, Carlos said, "It's terrific so many of us were able hear Dr. Chambers at the high school last month. Oh, and before we get started, who'd like to take notes tonight?"

As Tracy raised her hand, she said, "Since I'm sitting right next to the flipchart, I'll be glad to do it."

"Thanks," Carlos said to Tracy. Then he turned to the rest of us. "I thought what Dr. Chambers said was enlightening. I never thought about rewarding kids for learning, but now it makes sense. And, when I found out kids need both performance goals and learning goals, it blew my mind."

By the immediate reaction from the group seated around the living room, it was obvious people agreed with Carlos. I heard several people say, "Me, too," and "No kidding."

Pat raised her hand and said, "It's made a big impact in my classroom. I'd like to tell you about it."

"Go ahead," Carlos told her.

"Well, I had a class meeting and we talked about rewards," Pat explained. "The class was okay with not getting rewards, but they wanted to be recognized for what they learned. So we've decided to celebrate when we finish major units. Our first celebration is next week. This month each child read a biography of a famous person. The kids are going to dress up like the famous people and share what they've learned. Parents are coming and bringing snacks to help us celebrate."

Carlos said, "I'd like to be in your class, Pat."

I saw smiles on peoples' faces.

Carlos commented, "Dr. Chambers did say we could reward the *learning* instead of the result and that's what you're doing with the celebration."

Sandy asked, "Have you seen any changes in your class since you've stopped using rewards?"

"It's like night and day," Pat answered. "They are more cooperative and every single child is involved. They are having fun putting together their presentations and seem to be learning more because of it. There was no problem getting them to read the biographies either. The kids are proud of what they are *learning* and are eager to share.

Carlos said, "Thanks, Pat. I want to be in your class even more now! So, who wants to follow that act?"

Ben Lee stuck his hand up and said, "I've been working at getting my son, Greg, to be more interested in learning. He was having a hard time memorizing the states and capitals for a test, and I was spending hours trying to help him. As much as we worked, he wasn't learning, and it seemed I was the one who was frustrated over it."

"What did you do?" Carlos asked.

"I decided to take a new approach with Greg, and I definitely didn't offer him a reward."

There were a few snickers from the group.

"I said to myself 'Why am I stressing over this? Greg's the one who will be taking the test. So I asked him how he wanted to do on the test." Ben smiled as he put his hand up by his face and said, "I didn't tell him this would be his performance goal. Greg told me, 'If I get a B, I'll be happy.'"

"What did you think of that?" Carlos asked.

Ben smiled and continued, "I was okay with it because that was Greg's goal. But I also wanted Greg to take on the responsibility for learning. So, after he had his performance goal set, I asked him what *he* needed to do to learn the states and capitals."

Carlos jumped in, "That sounds good, Ben. Being responsible is a big part of a Can-Do Attitude."

Ben nodded. "But Greg said, 'I don't know, Dad. I've tried everything.' I could tell he didn't know how to study for the test. So I suggested breaking the states into small groups and learning a few each day. Greg liked that idea. He made a list of the states he still needed to learn and a time schedule. He had ten days and planned to learn four new states and their capitals each day."

"Isn't that called chunking?" Sandy asked who was sitting to our right.

"Yes, it is," Ben replied.

"Chunking? That's a funny word. I've never heard of that," Phil, who had been sitting quietly, said.

Sandy explained, "Well, Phil, chunking is when you take information and break it down into small, manageable chunks. I used chunking when I was studying to be a physician's assistant. It's a great way to keep from being overwhelmed." Sandy turned to Ben and asked, "How did it work for Greg?"

Ben laughed, "Beautifully! He got so into it, he came up with a fantastic idea for keeping track of his progress. He dug out an old states puzzle from second grade. Then, Greg took out all the states he didn't know.

Every time he learned a new state, he put it back into the puzzle."

"Sounds like a fun way to keep track!" Carlos said.

"It was. The learning goals seemed to take the pressure off Greg. Some days he didn't reach his daily goal, but other days he learned more than four, so it worked out. He was so proud of what he learned. As he began to fill up the puzzle, Greg would show it to us and say, 'Hey Mom and Dad, I know all these!' By the time the test came around, the puzzle was full."

"How did he do on the test?" Maggie asked.

"He did great. He got the grade he wanted, and the best part was he knew he did it himself. Now Greg is keeping track of all the states our family has been to on vacations. He's trying to talk us into going to the Four Corners this summer so he can stand on four states at one time."

The group laughed.

Carlos said, "Whoa, the way you did that with Greg sounds like it was part of a plan, Ben."

Ben said, "Thanks, but it wasn't planned. It just kind of fell into place logically. I was so pleased with the way it worked out that I put together a little formula for goal setting and brought a few copies with me."

"Super," Carlos said. "Can we see it?"

"Sure," Ben said as he picked up some papers from the table next to him and passed them around. "Oh, by the way, I decided to call this Can-Do Goal Setting."

Can-Do Goal Setting

1. Determine the performance goal.

2. Discuss together what needs to be learned to achieve the goal.

3. Break the information into manageable chunks.

4. Develop a plan for learning and a way to measure progress.

5. Give guidance, support, and encouragement as needed.

6. Acknowledge or celebrate learning and accomplishments.

"Wow!" Carlos said, holding up Ben's formula. "So, the trip to the Four Corners would be the celebration, right?"

Ben smiled and said, "That's what Greg has in mind. Min and I think it would be quite a family trip."

As I looked over what Ben wrote, it all followed his story with Greg and made sense. I could see how Ted and I might use it to do some goal setting with Chris. I heard people around me thanking Ben for writing up his formula and telling him how useful they thought it would be.

Carlos thanked Ben for all his work then said, "Why don't we take a break?"

Tracy asked, "Hey, Carlos, did you make your famous sugar cookies?"

Carlos smiled and said, "Just walk in the kitchen and you'll find out. There are other goodies and drinks, too. Why don't we come back in about fifteen minutes?"

It was funny to see how quickly people rushed into the kitchen. Ted was one of the first ones, and it wasn't long until he came back with a big cookie for me.

When the cookies were gone, everyone came back to the living room. I could tell Carlos enjoyed being the host that night, as several people asked for his cookie recipe. After promising to e-mail it with the night's notes, Carlos began by saying, "Dr. Chambers also talked about how important it is to make learning a way of life. Let's talk about that for a few minutes."

As hands went up all around us, I could tell the group had taken Dr. Chambers' words to heart. Carlos called on Maggie.

She said, "Like he suggested, I've started asking my girls what they've learned when they come home from school. It took a while to get going, but it's turned into a daily ritual now, and I don't even have to ask anymore. Jennie and Rachel can't wait to talk about what they've learned! And, I've found that I love talking to them about my day."

Tracy's husband, Jerome, who was also Chris's scout leader, was the next to talk. "I've been trying to make my son's learning relevant to his world. He wants a new pair of Adidas. Instead of just going out and buying them, I told him I would split the cost with him. So he's decided he's going to find the best price in town now that he's paying for half the shoes. He's spent hours reading the paper, on the internet, and calling to check prices. Guess what? He found the shoes for 40% off at an outlet."

After he finished speaking, Tracy added, "Our son has learned more about how to figure percentages in the past week than he ever thought possible. All of a sudden he understands the word 'Sale' and comparison shopping."

Carlos said, "It sounds like you all got it when Dr. Chambers said 'make learning a way of life.' So many people want to share, why don't we make a list of ways we can focus kids on learning?" He turned to Tracy who had already written the first two on the flipchart.

As people around the room shared their experiences, Tracy put down the main idea of each story on the flipchart.

This is the list she wrote.

> *Ways to Focus Kids on Learning*
>
> 1. *Use the Can-Do Goal Setting Formula.*
> 2. *Highlight learning more than grades by asking kids "What did you learn?"*
> 3. *Make what kids learn relevant to the world they live in.*
> 4. *Acknowledge what kids learn.*
> 5. *See mistakes as opportunities to learn.*
> 6. *Describe to kids what helped you learn.*
> 7. *Tell kids stories about famous people and what they went through to achieve success.*
> 8. *Share mistakes you made as a child.*
> 9. *Explain to kids the reasons for learning specific skills.*

Just as Tracy was writing down the last idea, a crack of thunder jolted the room.

"What was that?" Phil asked. At that moment, a flash of lightning lit up the yard outside the picture window.

The rain started coming down in buckets. I looked over at Ted, and he whispered to me, "I told you we didn't need that umbrella. By the way, Maggie just offered to give us a ride home."

Carlos began wrapping up the meeting. "We will e-mail you the list that Tracy wrote, plus my recipe," he said to the group. "Ted, didn't you want to say something about our final meeting for the year?"

Ted stood up and invited everyone to a Memorial Day family potluck at our house. He said, "I think it's time to acknowledge and celebrate all we have learned about parenting this year."

Everyone agreed and Ted told them we would call to find out who was coming and who wanted to bring what to eat.

The rain was still coming down hard when Ted picked up our umbrella from the hallway. He held it over me while we went down the front walk. Looking for Maggie's car on the dark wet street must have reminded Ted of an old movie because before I knew it, he was dancing and belting out, *"I'm Singing in the Rain..."* all the way to Maggie's car.

Chapter 18

We Can Do It!

*"How we parent our kids can make
a profound difference in their lives."*
-Phil McCoy

Ted and I couldn't believe it when we started calling people about the Memorial Day potluck. Everyone wanted to come! So, we decided to move the picnic to the park because we'd have plenty of people for a baseball game.

As I stood by the picnic tables that Memorial Day, I could see kids, parents, and grandparents all talking, playing, laughing, and goofing around. Even David Garcia and his wife, Anna, had come. It was going to be quite a celebration with over 30 people there.

The big event before the picnic was the baseball game. Both kids and parents had been looking forward to it all week. It was almost eleven o'clock in the morning before everyone had arrived, equipped with gloves, bats, and balls. After dropping off their dishes at the food table, the group gathered over at the baseball field.

Since there were 10 kids, we formed two teams, making sure there were 5 kids and 5 adults on each. Greg Lee and Jennie Stein offered to be the captains and drew the names out of hats—one for kids and the other for adults. Greg drew Rachel Stein, my Mom, Steve Moore, Min Lee, Kaitlin Moore, Jason Castelli, Carlos Hernandez, Jerome Johnson, and Mark Lee. They immediately named themselves The Goal Setters.

On Jennie's team was her mother, Phil McCoy, Chris, Pat Moore, Breanna Johnson, Ben Lee, Alex Moore, Tracy Johnson, and Andy Hernandez. Alex suggested naming the team The Connectors, and the rest of the team quickly agreed.

Mr. Garcia volunteered to be the umpire and flipped the coin. The Connectors won the toss and would be up to bat first. They piled into the dugout while The Goal Setters figured out who would play what position and then took their places on the field.

When Ted and I joined the spectators in the stands to watch the game, he commented, "Looks like there a plenty of *Number One Fans* here today!" Leave it to Ted to think of that.

There was a lot of chatter on the field from the Goal Setters. We heard, "Hey, batter. Hey, batter," coming from the enthused players as Breanna was first up to bat for The Connectors. She tried hard, but never even touched the ball with the bat. We didn't know if it was harder on Breanna or her Dad, Jerome, who was pitching.

Next up was Phil who got a hit, but never made it past first base. Pat, the third batter, walked to first base and Ted and I cheered when Chris was up next. He hit a fly ball to center field, right to his grandmother! When she caught it, Chris couldn't believe it and neither could Ted. I slapped him on the knee as I stood up and yelled, "Yea, Mom!"

Since that was the third out, the Goal Setters ran into their dugout and began warming up while the Connectors grabbed their gloves and ran out onto the field. The Goal Setters got two runs before three quick strikeouts.

By the beginning of the fourth inning, the score was still 2-0 in favor of the Goal Setters. As Maggie went up to bat, the fans started to chant for the Connectors. There was a loud chorus of "Earn that run! Earn that run! You Can Do It!"

At last, Maggie hit a wild one to the outfield and ran as fast as she could over first base, and slid into second base just before the ball got there. The next two batters, Ben and Jennie, both had hits, one to right field and the other to the short stop. But, the Goal Setters were too quick for them. Ben and Jennie were both put out at first base.

It was Andy's turn up at bat with two outs. As he made his way out of the dugout, his little face was peeking out underneath the batting helmet, and the bat he was carrying was almost as big as he was. We all smiled because in the second inning when Andy hit the ball, he ran the wrong way. Everyone got a chuckle out of it, when he ran to *third* base instead of first.

Now, as Andy made his way past the fence, I saw Sandy motioning her son over to her. From where we were sitting in the stands, Ted and I could hear her say to him, "The last time you hit the ball, Andy, you ran fast to third base."

Andy was beaming. Then, his mother asked, 'How come you didn't run to first base?"

Andy didn't blink an eye as he explained, "Cuz everyone who was going to first base got put out."

Sandy nodded her head. "Wow! You figured that out all by yourself, Andy." Andy was smiling as his mother went on, "This time, if you hit the ball and run to third base, you will be able to make it, but you won't be able to score."

Andy nodded slowly like he understood what his mother was telling him.

Sandy went on, "If you run to first base though, you might get put out, but you'll also have a chance to score. As the batter, it's your choice, Andy."

"Okay, Mommy," he said as he picked up the bat and walked over to home plate.

We watched as Andy made several practice swings and got in position for the first pitch. Jerome drew back his arm and threw a soft underhand throw right to Andy. When Andy's bat connected with the ball, the crowd cheered, and he took off running. His little legs were pumping as fast as they could all the way to first base. At the same instant, Maggie ran across home plate, scoring the first run for the Connectors. The crowd went wild.

Sandy was jumping up and down in front of us like a proud mother. Ted leaned over and said to her, "Sounds like that Can-Do Feedback paid off, Mom!" It was Sandy's turn to beam.

By top of the eighth inning, the score was tied 5 to 5. Breanna was coming up to bat again for the Connectors. As she trudged out of the dugout, she looked like she'd lost her best friend. She had struck out both times she'd been up at bat. Even her dad, Jerome, looked pained at his daughter's misery.

Breanna's grandmother was sitting right next to us. "I sure hope Breanna at least hits the ball this time," she said shaking her head. "This is the first baseball game she's ever played. When she found out there was going to be a game, she asked Jerome to teach her how to hit. They've been practicing in the backyard every night. But, she was so nervous about playing today."

Ted said, "She's pretty brave to be out there playing for the first time."

We saw Jerome smile at Breanna as she was standing next to home plate with the bat dragging in the dirt. Just then, Jerome did a little tap dance step on the pitcher's mound. Ted almost fell off his seat laughing.

Breanna's grandmother smiled and explained, "That's what he does to get Breanna to stop worrying so much. She gets so caught up in doing things right, it practically paralyzes her. She taught her Daddy that dance step, and he does it to remind her to have fun and that she's still learning how to play baseball."

After seeing what her Dad did, an immediate change seemed to come over Breanna. She picked up the bat, straightened her shoulders and got ready for the first pitch.

Jerome threw the ball, and Breanna swung the bat, and it swooshed through the air. "Strike!" came from Mr. Garcia. Breanna stayed right in there, as the next pitch went outside. "Ball!" yelled, Mr. Garcia.

Breanna got ready again, and this time when the ball came over home plate, she swung with all her might. We heard the snap and watched the ball fly up over her Dad's head, past the short stop and into the outfield.

Breanna stood there for a moment, looking shocked. "Run, Breanna, run," her Dad was shouting from the pitcher's mound.

All of a sudden, Breanna headed for first base, making it before the outfielder could get the ball there. Jumping up and down on the base, she yelled, "I did it!" We all clapped, and her grandmother was on her feet, cheering the loudest of all.

When the game ended in a 6-5 win for the Connectors, the parents and grandparents in the stands clapped and cheered for both teams. It was funny to hear the Can-Do recognition going on around us.

Tracy said to Breanna, "Hey, all that practice with your Dad paid off!"

Maggie's new boyfriend, Bill, had been in the stands with us. The girls and Maggie brought him over to meet us. After we shook hands, Jennie said to her mother, "I'm so glad you were on our team, Mom. Your first run inspired the whole team to try harder."

I heard Carlos tell Andy, "When you ran to first base, it sure helped the team. Because you did that, Maggie could run to home plate and score. Way to go, Andy," his dad said as he picked up his son and put him on his shoulders.

Chris came running over to Ted and me, with a huge smile on his face. He said, "When we had so many strike outs, we thought we'd never get a hit. We were ready to give up."

"What changed?" Ted asked.

"In the dugout Alex told us 'All we need to do is work a little harder.' So, we practiced hitting, pitching and running behind the dugout."

So that's where they had been. "No wonder the

dugout looked so empty when you guys were up at bat," I said. "You were practicing. Mastering a skill takes work."

Chris nodded, "I know, and I'm glad we did it. I'm so hungry. When do we eat, Mom?"

I put my arm around him, and together we walked over to the picnic area, still talking about the game.

When Ted, Jerome, and Tracy started putting the chicken and hamburgers on the grill, Phil, my mother and I organized all the different types of food people had brought. The kids got busy spreading out and taping down paper tablecloths on the picnic tables.

The smell of the hamburgers and chicken sizzling on the grill drifted through the hungry crowd. It wasn't long before Ted put the first plate of cooked burgers and chicken on the table and the line at the food table formed.

Pretty soon everyone was seated and the feasting began. The happy chatter gave way to silence as everyone concentrated on chowing down. As soon as the kids finished eating, they ran back to the baseball field.

When I returned from the dessert table with a slice of apple pie, Ted started humming a few bars of the National Anthem. As he took a bite of my pie he said, "This is just a little too much—apple pie, mom, and baseball!"

"And to think I gave up my weekly golf game with the guys for this," Steve said laughing. Then he got a serious expression on his face. "I wouldn't have missed being here with everyone today. I truly think the open talking and sharing about our parenting ups and downs over the past months has helped all of us."

Pat smiled at her husband's comment. "And, it's changed the atmosphere in my classroom, too. What we've read and discussed has given me the confidence to try new ways to relate with kids. It has certainly made my job easier and more enjoyable."

"I never thought I'd see the day, but Chris is actually sad to see the end of the school year coming," I told everyone at the table. "He's started enjoying learning, even though he knows he has to work at it."

Phil said, "What this all says to me is how we parent our kids can makes a profound difference in their lives. And, I'd forgotten parenting is just plain work! This group has helped me raise my grandson this year."

Tracy spoke up, "Now that I know what it takes, parenting is actually easier, and I look forward to helping Breanna have a Can-Do Attitude." She looked at Jerome and patted his arm. "We can do it." Jerome nodded in agreement.

Ted said, "Yeah, we can do it." And pretty soon everyone around us was saying it, too.

As I watched and listened to everyone, I thought, you know, Maggie was right when she said, "No one ever told me having kids was so much fun!"

Appendix

PROBLEM SOLVING PROCESS (PSP)

1. <u>Just the facts! (Without criticism or blame)</u>

2. <u>What caused this to happen?</u>

3. <u>What are possible options?</u>

4. <u>What will affect the solution?</u>

5. <u>What's the best solution? *(Is it possible and appropriate?)*</u>

6. <u>Carry it out and evaluate results – did it work or not?</u>

Evaluation

Things to work on:

Bibliography

Bandura, Albert, *Self-Efficacy: The Exercise of Control.* New York: W.H. Freeman and Company, 1998.

Calkins, Lucy with Lydia Bellino, *Raising Lifelong Learners: A Parent's Guide.* Cambridge, Massachusetts: Perseus Books, 1998.

Canfield, Jack, *Chicken Soup for the Soul.* Deerfield, FL: Health Communications, Inc., 1999.

Cline, Foster and Jim Fay, *Parenting with Love and Logic: Teaching Children Responsibility.* Colorado Springs, Colorado: Pinion Press, 1990.

Covey, Stephen R., *The 7 Habits of Highly Effective People: Powerful Lessons in Personal Change.* New York: Simon and Schuster, 1990.

Csikszentmihalyi, Mihaly, *Finding Flow: The Psychology of Engagement With Everyday Life.* New York: Harper Collins, 1997.

Csikszentmihalyi, Mihaly, *Flow: The Psychology of Optimal Experience.* New York: Harper Collins, 1990.

Dweck, Carol, *Self-Theories: Their Role in Motivation, Personality, and Development.* Philadelphia: Psychology Press, 2000.

Faber, Adele and Elaine Mazlish, *How To Talk So Kids Can Learn.* New York: Simon and Schuster, 1996.

Faber, Adele and Elaine Mazlish, *How To Talk So Kids Will Listen & Listen So Kids Will Talk.* New York: Avon Books, 1999.

Ginott, Haim G., *Between Parent and Child.* New York: Avon Books, 1969.

Goleman, Daniel and Richard Boyatzis and Annie McKee, *Primal Leadership: Realizing The Power Of Emotional Intelligence.* Boston: Harvard Business School Press, 2002.

Gordon, Thomas, *Parent Effectiveness Training: The Proven Program for Raising Responsible Children.* New York: Three Rivers Press, 2000.

Gottman, John and Joan DeClaire, *The Heart of Parenting: How To Raise An Emotionally Intelligent Child.* New York: Simon and Schuster, 1997.

Kohn, Alfie, *Beyond Discipline: From Compliance to Community.* Alexandria, VA: Association For Supervision and Curriculum Development, 1996.

Kohn, Alfie, *Punished by Rewards: The Trouble with Gold Stars, Incentive Plans, A's, Praise, and Other Bribes.* New York: Houghton Mifflin Company, 1993.

Kouzes, James M. and Barry Z. Posner, *Encouraging The Heart: A Leader's Guide To Rewarding And Recognizing Others.* San Francisco: Jossey-Bass Inc. Publishers, 1999.

Reivich, Karen and Andrew Shatte, *The Resilience Factor: 7 Keys to Finding Your Inner Strength and Overcoming Life's Hurdles.* New York: Broadway Books, 2002.

Seligman, Martin E. P., *Authentic Happiness: Using the New Positive Psychology to Realize Your Potential for Lasting Fulfillment.* New York: Free Press, 2002.

Seligman, Martin E. P. with Karen Reivich, Lisa Jaycox, and Jane Gillham, *The Optimistic Child: A Proven Program to Safeguard Children Against Depression and Build Lifelong Resilience.* New York: Harper Collins Publishers, 1995.

Stipek, Deborah and Kathy Seal, *Motivated Minds: Raising Children to Love Learning.* New York: Henry Holt and Company, 2001.

How to Order More Books

CALL: (760) 771-9818
or
FAX this order form to (775) 373-0534

Please send me _____ copies of "I Can Do It!"

Enclosed is $17.95 per book   _____

California residents add 7.75% sales tax   _____

Shipping & handling: $4.00 for first book,
Plus $2.00 for each additional book   _____

Total Enclosed: _____

Mail books to: _____

_____

_____

_____

Enclosed is my check in the amount of: _____

For other inquiries, to have us speak at one of your functions, for guidelines on setting up your own Can-Do Parent Group, please contact us at:
Website: www.candokid.com
E-Mail: mblockeducate@aol.com
E-Mail: pamgolden@aol.com

Thank you!

We give discounts when ordering more than 10 books.